Cambridge Elements ≡

Elements in Religion and Monotheism
edited by
Paul K. Moser
Loyola University Chicago
Chad Meister
Bethel University

T0287086

MONOTHEISM AND THE RISE OF SCIENCE

J. L. Schellenberg
Mount Saint Vincent University

CAMBRIDGE
UNIVERSITY PRESS

CAMBRIDGE
UNIVERSITY PRESS

University Printing House, Cambridge CB2 8BS, United Kingdom

One Liberty Plaza, 20th Floor, New York, NY 10006, USA

477 Williamstown Road, Port Melbourne, VIC 3207, Australia

314–321, 3rd Floor, Plot 3, Splendor Forum, Jasola District Centre, New Delhi – 110025, India

79 Anson Road, #06–04/06, Singapore 079906

Cambridge University Press is part of the University of Cambridge.

It furthers the University's mission by disseminating knowledge in the pursuit of education, learning, and research at the highest international levels of excellence.

www.cambridge.org
Information on this title: www.cambridge.org/9781108794909
DOI: 10.1017/9781108889094

First published 2020

A catalogue record for this publication is available from the British Library.

ISBN 978-1-108-79490-9 Paperback
ISSN 2631-3014 (online)
ISSN 2631-3006 (print)

Monotheism and the Rise of Science

Elements in Religion and Monotheism

DOI: 10.1017/9781108889094
First published online: November 2020

J. L. Schellenberg
Mount Saint Vincent University
Author for correspondence: J. L. Schellenberg, john.schellenberg@msvu.ca

Abstract: This Element traces the effects of science's rise on the cultural status of monotheism. Starting in the past, it shows how monotheism contributed to science's rise, and how, returning the favour, science provided aid and support, until fairly recently, for the continuing success of monotheism in the West. Turning to the present, the Element explores reasons for supposing that explanatorily, and even on an existential level, science is taking over monotheism's traditional roles in Western culture. These reasons are found to be less powerful than is commonly supposed, though the existential challenge can be made effective when framed in an unusual and indirect manner. Finally, the Element considers how the relationship between science's high standing and the status of monotheism might appear in the future. Could something like monotheism rise again, and might science help it do so? The Element concludes that an affirmative answer is possible.

Keywords: science, monotheism, religion, status, past, present, future

ISBNs: 9781108794909 (PB), 9781108889094 (OC)
ISSNs: 2631–3014 (online), 2631–3006 (print)

Contents

1 Aims and Terms

1.1 Aims

Science, as everyone knows, has through its many wonder-inducing activities attained a position of eminence in our culture. In this Element I will trace the effects of science's rise on the cultural status of a religious idea known as monotheism – the idea that there is exactly one God, supreme over all. The Element does not address normative issues about whether monotheism or something like monotheism is true or rationally believed. I have discussed such issues in other writing, but here the aim is just to get clearer about what belongs to and may yet appear in a certain layer, as it were, of cultural evolution, by thinking about past, present, and future in turn.

How the cultural status of science affects that of monotheism now – today – naturally gets a lot of attention from those who think about such things. Many would say that science's steady rise and sustained prominence have greatly weakened monotheism's hold on cultural power in the West. Explanatorily, and even on an existential level, a scientific approach to life is in effect replacing monotheism in our culture. Or so it is often thought. I will explain these views and offer an assessment.

But before coming to that issue, which is about the present, I wish to address some issues about the past that allow us to consider the possibility that, however things may be today between monotheism and science, they have not always been contentious. It is sometimes said that monotheism's cultural dominance in the Europe of the seventeenth century contributed to science's early rise by, for example, generating presuppositions favourable to the scientific exploration of nature. Much less often do we hear about science's subsequent cultural standing providing aid and support, until fairly recently, for the continuing success of monotheism in the West. As it turns out, there are interesting arguments for both suggestions. I shall assess their force.

Then also, on the *other* side of the obvious question about the present, I aim to consider how the relationship between science's high standing and the status of monotheism might appear in the future. Of course, when dealing with the future, one has little to go on. I shall give the more positive possibilities a chance here too, though, asking whether there are scientific results we have been taught to honour that, when applied in the right way, might help monotheism evolve in such a way as to be once more a significant cultural player. Could something like monotheism rise again, and might science help it do so? I will seek to answer these questions.

Because my treatment of monotheism's prospects is not unfriendly, some who reach the end of this Element may wonder whether what they have been reading is itself a religious work – perhaps a new sort of natural theology? My thought earlier about a shelving of normative issues is relevant at this point. But let me add a thought that may be more informative. One of the tasks of the most openminded and impartial inquiry, alive to all that may remain unseen as well as our human infirmities, is to bring to light overlooked or neglected possibilities and then invite further discussion instead of offering final pronouncements. Here as elsewhere, I am enthusiastically committed to this task.

1.2 Terms

So much for my aims. Let me now clarify some terms. *Science* I shall take broadly, as referring to the intellectual tradition focused on understanding the natural world that (with significant precursors in ancient Egypt and Mesopotamia) had its beginnings among the ancient Greeks, was ably represented by Muslim scholars in the medieval period, and most importantly is associated with what we call modern science. *Modern science*, in common with other writers, I shall take as referring to the distinctive part of this tradition that goes back to the flowering of scientific inquiry in Europe during the century and a half after Copernicus published his heliocentric astronomy in 1543, a time when scientists were still called natural philosophers. This period is of course the one often designated as hosting the 'scientific revolution'. Though a small part of it belongs to the sixteenth century, I shall follow the usual practice, which is to speak of the scientific revolution as a seventeenth-century phenomenon.

Cultural status (a term I treat synonymously with *cultural standing*, *cultural position*, and *cultural power*) will here mean the degree of prestige – that is, respect or admiration – and influence enjoyed by an idea or movement or tradition in some cultural context. Cultural status, as here understood, clearly cannot be quantified in any precise manner, but we can still have reason to speak of the cultural status of monotheism or science in the West as high or low or growing or diminishing. And for our purposes that will be sufficient. By the *rise* of science or of monotheism I shall mean an increase in its cultural status and especially (for science) the striking growth in cultural power realized in and after the seventeenth century. It is worth noting that our focus will usually be on Western culture, since it is in this part of human culture that science arose and monotheism once dominated, and it is here, more recently, that the 'religion wars' and debates about 'science and religion' have been most pronounced. Of course, it is also often easier to make reliable claims about cultural developments when one's focus is thus restricted.

What about religious terms? Let us start with *theism*, which I define quite generally as referring to the claim (or statement or proposition or view or idea) that there is at least one god. More specific types of theism are generated if we add to this claim the claim that two or more gods warrant our attention (this view is called *polytheism*) or add the claim that there is just one, holding that it is the only god that exists and thus God (*monotheism*). Considering only the content of the latter claim, we would be hard pressed to say why the claim that everything is God, known as *pantheism*, should not be regarded as a form of monotheism. After all, pantheism is a form of theism, and entails that there is just one divine reality. Towards the end of the Element we will have reason to entertain such thoughts further, but for now I will go along with the assumption, common both in the literature and in non-academic religious discourse, that the single God of monotheism is to be distinguished from other things, including any universe, and is not, as pantheism would have it, to be viewed as the sole reality.

Sometimes such god-related terms as I have listed here are used to refer not just to claims but also to more complex sets of things, including belief of these claims and corresponding forms of worship. So it is important to note that mine is a narrower or simpler usage in this respect. Especially today, it is the *claim* monotheists make that is the focus of intellectual discussion and that is thought to be challenged by the rise of science, so I have elected to chart the fortunes of this claim through time in relation to science's own fortunes. But corresponding forms of belief and worship will not be entirely left aside, since part of the influence of monotheism as I am understanding it comes precisely in the extent to which it elicits belief and worship.

In contemporary philosophy the term *theism* is often used in a manner that diverges from my usage here: to refer, specifically, to the claim that there is a personal deity or divine being who is omnipotent, omniscient, and omnibenevolent. This philosopher's theism can, however, quite easily be converted into something compatible with my usage by labelling it *omnitheism*. *Omnitheism* overlaps with *monotheism*, since the omni-concept that philosophers have developed is plausibly seen as implicit in the claims about God made in Judaism, Christianity, and Islam – the traditions that have shepherded the monotheistic idea from the time of its Hebrew origin until now.[1]

But there is still something to distinguish my use of *monotheism* from the philosophical *omnitheism*. Contexts in which the former term is used are often ones in which the history of God talk – more on this in a moment – is relevant in a way it generally is not relevant in situations involving omnitheism, and in which the themes of unity, universality, and ultimacy, as applied to the divine, figure more prominently. The discussion of this Element will be another such context.

---

[1] Its Hebrew origin, by the way, we should distinguish from its origin *simpliciter*, since there are Greek and Egyptian precursors. On this see, for example, Kirk et al. (1983) and Hoffmeier (2015).

In scholarly historical work, monotheism, which affirms that no god other than the favoured one exists, is commonly distinguished from henotheism, which favours one God among others whose co-existence is granted. The history of God-related talk and other religious behaviour is often seen as involving stages of polytheism, henotheism, and monotheism – though these are not always presented as coming neatly in that order. In such discussions henotheism, like the other theisms, is commonly depicted as involving a certain form of worship, but, as noted, I will not follow this precedent, focusing instead on what is being claimed. So if the term *henotheism* is to make an appearance in the present context, we will need a claim to go with it. By looking for one, incidentally, we accommodate another complexity of usage, which is that in some scholarly work the term *monolatry* replaces *henotheism*. The former clearly refers to a form of worship – worship of one God while in some way countenancing the existence of others. So by treating henotheism as a claim, we can give the corresponding term a job to do that has not already been taken over by *monolatry*. What claim should it be? I suggest we think of henotheism as the claim that one god deserves our attention more than others do, even though other gods also exist. Henotheism, as a claim, thus falls at a point intermediate between polytheism and monotheism. In the next section of this Element, which begins our tour through time by directing our attention to contact between science and monotheism in the past, we will have occasion to revisit not just monotheism but these other, alternative religious views as well.

2 Did Monotheism Benefit from Science's Rise?

As I mentioned in Section 1, that monotheism had by the seventeenth century become culturally entrenched in Europe is often said to have contributed to science's early rise. There is considerable support for such claims, and I will now detail some of this. But then I will move on to an issue almost never broached: did science subsequently *return* the favour by aiding and protecting monotheism?

2.1 How Monotheism Aided Science

We may begin by noticing that the cultural heft of monotheism afforded a kind of *negative* support for the rise of science by preventing what would have been an obstacle to it, namely widespread belief in the existence of multiple gods at work in nature. Monotheism helped, we might say, simply by *not* being polytheism or henotheism. Already during an earlier period of scientific development, in ancient Greece, advances in thinking about material causes were seen to depend on achieving some distance from the idea of interfering gods (Deming 2010, 17). Had the habit of linking mundane events to the decisions of gods been culturally dominant in the seventeenth century, the explanatory power of a focus on mundane physical agencies quite without intentions or intentionality – on the causal properties inherent in physical things – might not have made itself known and would at least have been more difficult to see. Monotheism's high standing, culturally speaking, was sufficient to prevent such science-unfriendly conditions from obtaining.

But God too is a god, someone may say, so how exactly were things more science-friendly in a monotheistic cultural environment? Actually, the differences between 'God' and 'god' are very important here, given how the former was construed. Indeed, these differences allowed monotheism to be a good deal more science-friendly than we have yet seen, to afford not just the negative, obstacle-removing support we have been talking about – which, as you may have noticed, is compatible with monotheism itself constituting a different sort of obstacle – but also *positive* support for the rise of science.

This occurred quite contingently, because of certain features of the monotheism that was in fact influential in the Europe of the seventeenth century. Aristotle's monotheism, had it been culturally dominant then, would probably not have had the same effects, since along with it came a partitioned cosmos – perfect spheres beyond the moon and a corrupt sublunar sphere – that was inimical to the notion of universal laws of nature (Brooke 1991, 52–3). Indeed, some have argued that it was precisely because the Bishop of Paris in the 1270s *condemned* a host of Aristotelian claims, including the claim that God could not create multiple universes or move the universe in a straight line, substituting an emphasis on divine freedom associated with Catholic monotheism, that important space opened up for new scientific explorations later on (Lindberg 2002, 69). Others have said that it is particular features of Protestant Christian monotheism in the seventeenth century – perhaps its encouragement of a naturalistic reading of the 'book of nature' parallel to the literalism Protestants applied to the 'book of Scripture' – that we have to thank for the emergence of modern science (Harrison 1998). But without going into these specialized debates, whose issues are controversial, we can see a clear example of how monotheism was helpful by reflecting on certain broad and broadly influential monotheistic *presuppositions* that were encouraging to scientific activity.

By a 'presupposition' I here mean a widely imbibed picture of things that helps to shape the thought of a culture, that lies behind or reinforces the intellectual directions it takes, often in ways the people of that culture do not consciously recognize.[2] Notice that I only say 'helps' and 'lies behind or reinforces' – the

---

[2] Saying that a presupposition has this causal power, it should be noted, does not commit us to the view that without its help things could not have fallen out much as they did – that in possible worlds relevantly similar to the actual in which such a presupposition is not present, what it

relevant picture of things need not be conceived as doing the whole causal job all by itself. Three monotheistic ideas can be seen as presuppositions in this sense in relation to the cultural direction represented by modern science: God as rational law-giver; God as a personal being not entirely unlike ourselves, with whose mind ours has affinities; and God as omnipotent Creator. These three ideas contributed to the apparent plausibility of three highly significant assumptions animating modern science – assumptions not always sufficiently distinguished. Respectively, these are that there exist natural *laws*, that the order represented by these laws is *intelligible*, and that all of nature is *unified* by this lawlike order, which is exhibited everywhere in it, from head to toe.

Let us take these assumptions one at a time and consider their connections to monotheism, starting with lawlike order in nature. Immediately we face an objection. Monotheism, it may be suggested, was not at all needed for this idea. Already in various of the philosophical schools of ancient Greece, and not only in such as were incipiently or actually monotheistic, the idea of nature's rational order was celebrated. The approach of the Stoics was one such, and the Stoics' God is immanent in nature, not its transcendent creator.

However, it is one thing for something like the Stoic idea to be, as it were, in the intellectual wind, and another for it to be actively determining things on the ground in the period leading up to science's early rise in and after the seventeenth century in Europe. We do hear from Alfred North Whitehead that 'the most effective way in which the Stoics influenced the mentality of the Middle Ages was by the diffused sense of order which arose from Roman law' (Whitehead 1929, 14). And Paul Davies tells us that a 'strongly enforced concept of civil law' in medieval Europe had something to do with the emergence of the scientific idea of laws of nature (Davies 1992, 76). So we may suppose that Stoic ideas were finding some relevant work to do. But according to Davies, that is just one part of the story. Drawing on John Barrow's pioneering work on the history of our conception of laws of nature (Barrow 1988), Davies argues that 'the Christian doctrine of God's law manifested in nature' also played a significant role. The presuppositional influence of the latter notion is confirmed when we notice, as Davies does, that the astronomers Tycho Brahe and Johannes Kepler, when working out the laws of planetary motion, and also Isaac Newton, whose laws of motion and gravitation were of course absolutely central to the rise of science, 'believed that in studying the orderly processes of nature they were uncovering God's rational design' (Davies 1992, 76). And these are just a few striking examples among many we might contemplate. Later

actually aids (e.g. some aspect of modern science) is commensurately *lacking* in assistance. Other conditions could, in some different way, provide this help in worlds where monotheism does not.

scientists would grow up singing about this sentiment in church, as John Kempthorne's 1796 hymn *Praise the Lord, Ye Heavens Adore Him* shows:

> Praise the Lord! For he hath spoken
> Worlds his mighty voice obeyed
> Laws, which never shall be broken
> For their guidance He hath made.

That natural philosophers or scientists saw themselves as uncovering *God's* laws is even more important when we come to the second central assumption of science, which concerns the intelligibility of nature – the assumption that nature's structure is open to the human gaze, that it can be *understood* by questing human minds if the right sorts of effort are brought to bear. On the monotheistic picture, natural laws are chosen by a personal divine being, not inherent in nature as many Greek thinkers including the Stoics assumed. Thus so long as our mindedness and personhood have some affinities with God's, and God is willing for God's ways to become known to us, we may have confidence that the study of nature will produce reliable results. And precisely this basis for confidence was offered by the theological presupposition at work in this second case.

For Whitehead, this is the point to be emphasized, and he does so eloquently. The conviction of intelligibility was 'vividly implanted in the European mind' by a picture of God that combined 'the personal energy of Jehovah' with 'the rationality of a Greek philosopher'. Whitehead says that he is talking about 'the impress on the European mind arising from the unquestioned faith of centuries'; in other words, a monotheistic presupposition. He concludes that the assumption of intelligibility – the sense of 'a secret that can be unveiled' in the absence of which 'the incredible labours of scientists would be without hope' – is 'an unconscious derivative of medieval theology' (Whitehead 1929, 15–16).

Other more recent writers have agreed (Brooke 1991, 19; Davis and Winship 2002, 123; Osler 2002, 148; Henry 2010, 53). There is even reason to think that support for the experimental method – this *way* of making nature's laws intelligible – was generated by monotheistic theology. That is because those who emphasized God's free imposition of laws ('voluntarists', as they are known) held that God could create and design things in any way at all, and so human investigators needed to get out and experience nature to determine how God's choices were actually made (Wilson 2002, 20). But here the contingency of such historical connections between monotheism and science must again be stressed. The voluntarist emphasis on the omnipotence and freedom of God, taken too far, could instead have been a disincentive to science. This has, from time to time, been a temptation for thinkers from various monotheistic traditions. Consider, for example, the view of the tenth-century Sunni Muslim thinker al-Ash'ari, who sharply restricted and indeed entirely denied natural causal agency in the name of the same divine properties, 'holding that God was the only and direct cause of all events, even of human actions' (Dhanani 2002, 85). Such an emphasis on divine causes could certainly distract one from the thought of natural ones, and in this way, somewhat ironically, we would be back to worries very like those emphasized earlier in connection with polytheism and henotheism. Clearly, it is rather important that when theological voluntarism made an appearance in seventeenth-century Europe, it generally did not take this extreme form.

What about the third assumption critical to the rise of science, that nature is *unified* by its lawlike structure? Here we have a rather important bundle of ideas: about natural laws that hold universally, that are interwoven in their operation, and perhaps also gathered under some highest law – which today we might associate with a 'theory of everything'. The third monotheistic presupposition, of God as omnipotent creator, was well suited to support these ideas about the unity of nature. For as the all-powerful creator, God alone is responsible for the existence and character of everything else. And a single rational Lawmaker in charge of everything may be expected to work according to a unifying plan.

The pioneers of science agreed. As Descartes said, we can expect a more perfect overall structure or organization for the various parts of a building 'on which one man alone has worked' than for a building whose construction had many masters (Descartes 1954, 296). In a similar vein, Isaac Newton wrote: 'If there be an universal life and all space be the sensorium of a thinking being who by immediate presence perceives all things in it . . . the laws of motion arising from life will or may be of universal extent' (quoted in Westfall 1971, 397). God not only is responsible for natural laws and their intelligibility, Europeans of the seventeenth century were inclined to think, but also impresses a lawlike structure on the *whole* of nature. This idea fed a belief in the unity of nature, which in turn has fed science.

2.2 How Science Aided Monotheism

That the rise of science was to some extent aided by the cultural dominance of monotheism in seventeenth-century Europe is therefore clear. And there are other forms of this aid that we have not mentioned. The esteemed historian of science, John Hedley Brooke, points out that not just monotheistic presuppositions but also monotheistic sanctions and motives were operative in the seventeenth century and encouraging to scientific activity (Brooke 1991, 19–33). However, it is time for us to move on. An interesting question awaits: did monotheism during and after the scientific revolution receive any *returns* on its investment in scientific thinking? Was it benefited by science's early rise? This question's interest derives in part from its answer, which is affirmative. A crass but popular view of the history of religion and science would have it that as soon as science gained in cultural standing, monotheism began a long trek out of cultural favour. But this view is mistaken. Monotheism's cultural status was instead maintained for a considerable period, and support gleaned from the rise of science was a part of the cause.

Once again we have both negative and positive support, though in the latter case there is a reversal: while, as we have seen, it took certain specific forms of monotheism to generate aid for science, when science returned the favour it was generally not this or that specific form of monotheism that benefited but rather the general idea of a single ultimate divinity. I will begin here by developing the second half of this point, concerning positive support.

Monotheism, considered under the aspect of a theory, can be seen as 'predicting' that the world of nature will be found to have certain features suggested by the character of the monotheistic deity. And what science did was to provide striking confirmation for these predictions. Thus it enabled monotheism to claim support from science for its central claims.[3] Naturally few *detailed* predictions of the sort generated by, say, a Lutheran Protestant Christian *version* of monotheism would have been viewed as confirmed, but the general ideas associated with the unity and wisdom and even benevolence of the divine were made to appear more plausible by reference to science's success at showing the world to be just as we should expect it to be if they were true. Central here was the lawlike structure of the natural world laid bare by science and certain particular features of the world thus displayed. A powerful tradition of natural theology grew up around such results which was to hold sway among European minds until scepticism induced by Darwinism, along with certain associated cultural events, began to dilute its effects around the end of the nineteenth century.

Charles Darwin himself, in his university years, experienced the persuasive power of science-fed natural theology. In his autobiography (Darwin 1958), written towards the end of his life, he reflected on how entranced he had been by William Paley's clever design arguments, which appealed to innumerable details unearthed by natural philosophers suggesting a beautiful providential adaptation of creatures to their environment. 'Just as we might expect if there really were a God!' one can almost hear Paley cry over and over again as one

---

[3] Of course, as we have seen, monotheism earlier supported the attempt to do work including such confirmation! If a troublesome circularity appears to loom, remember that our aim is not to determine the extent of actual objective rational support for monotheism afforded by the rise of science but to describe how the effects of the latter were viewed and how monotheism's cultural status waxed or waned accordingly.

reads his *Natural Theology*. Perhaps not quite the omnitheism of the philo-sophers is being supported here, but certainly it is belief in a single divine reality with highly impressive qualities. For Paley, the works of creation testify to a wisdom far surpassing any with which we are acquainted (Paley 1809, 445). Here are some of his chapter titles: 'Of the vessels of animal bodies', 'Comparative anatomy', 'Of insects', 'Of plants'. Benevolence is shown by the fact that where 'contrivance' – one of Paley's favourite words – is perceived, it tends to produce benefit, and by the pleasure that, without any apparent purpose, commonly attends animal sensations. Bees and flies, he commented, seemed far happier as they whirled through the sky than they had any reason to be (Paley 1809, 454–7). The unity of the deity was proven by the uniformity of the plan natural philosophers had observed in the universe. 'One principle of gravitation causes a stone to drop toward the earth, and the moon to wheel round it . . .. The light from a fixed star affects our eyes in the same manner, is refracted and reflected according to the same laws, as the light of a candle' (Paley 1809, 449–50). The young Darwin was 'charmed and convinced by the long line of argumentation' (Darwin 1958, 59).

Of course, as the older Darwin goes on to observe perhaps somewhat ruefully in his autobiography, much of Paley's design argumentation had now been put in the shade by his own discovery of natural selection. He was no longer convinced. But it is interesting to note how even some scientific discoveries later associated with evolutionary theory, and indeed even certain aspects of Darwin's own discovery, could be seen and were seen as supporting monotheistic ideas. Here is one of the first palaeontologists, the nineteenth-century scientist William Buckland, on fossil finds: [T]he discov-ery, amid the relics of past creations, of links that seemed wanting in the present system of organic nature, affords to natural Theology an important argument, in proving the unity and universal agency of a common great first cause' (quoted in Rupke 1983, 173). And Darwin's friend in America, Asa Gray, put into a textbook his thought that the divergence of biological species from a common ancestor, as shown by Darwin, was evidence that they are 'all part of one system', natural instantiations of 'the conception of One Mind' (Gray 1887, 177).

I have referred to predictions of theism shown to be successful by science. On the other side of the coin we have *failed* predictions of *non*-monotheistic notions such as polytheism, and I shall conclude this discussion of science's positive support of monotheism with an example. The tradition of natural theology represented by Paley has survived into the present day, and my example comes from its most celebrated contemporary exponent, Richard Swinburne. Swinburne argues that we should explain the existence of our universe by reference to 'one being who is the cause of the existence of all others'. Polytheism, he says, would have a harder time accounting for the sort of universe we have:

> If there were more than one deity responsible for the order of the universe, we would expect to see characteristic marks of the handiwork of different deities in different parts of the universe, just as we see different kinds of workmanship in the different houses of a city. We would expect to find an inverse square law of gravitation obeyed in one part of the universe, and in another part a law that was just short of being an inverse square law – without the difference being explicable in terms of a more general law. (Swinburne 2004, 147)

And of course this expectation is not fulfilled. As Swinburne adds, ours is 'a universe governed throughout space and time by the same natural laws' (Swinburne 2004, 147).

So much for positive support from the rise of science for the flourishing of monotheistic ideas. What about the negative support referred to earlier? What exactly is this? Recall that before we saw how a culturally ascendant polytheism or henotheism in the Europe of the seventeenth century would have prevented or complicated science's rise, and how monotheism's standing meant that this threat was altogether avoided. Monotheism helped because it was not polytheism or henotheism. Similarly, a renewed emphasis on polytheistic or henotheistic ideas, or the advent and cultural success of some other religious idea emphasizing the divine in nature, would have diminished monotheism's high status or complicated its retention at any time during the centuries following the scientific revolution, and the success of science aided in the avoidance of this threat. Science helped because it was unfriendly to such developments. Science's rise, given the emphasis that came with it on impersonal material causes operating throughout the natural world, made it harder for religious claims with implications for the natural world running contrary to this emphasis to take root and flourish in a manner threatening to monotheism's cultural status during the time in question. It was a bulwark against the resurgence of monotheism's main rivals.

Someone may now object, however, that the bulwark science represented was not a necessary condition of monotheism's continued success or in any other way critical to the obtaining of this cultural fact. Having already achieved cultural success – a high cultural standing – by the seventeenth century, quite independent factors were in play to help keep monotheism dominant thereafter: take, for example, the many powerful institutions presupposing Christian belief – not least, of course, the Church! Thus science's help wasn't really needed. But this point should not prevent us from seeing that, in the manner I have described, science was indeed for some considerable time on side with monotheism, and favourably orientated towards it. Going back to the metaphor of a bulwark: if six bulwarks separate invaders from a castle and they are stopped by the fifth, it is still correct to say that the sixth was defending the castle and making it harder for the invaders to get in. Extra support or unnecessary support is still support.

A more important point, perhaps, is that we do not really know how things would have gone *without* modern science. Imagine it cut out of history. Given a properly historical sensibility, one should allow that new cultural factors opposing monotheism and favouring one of its religious rivals might now find room to blossom. Stranger things have happened, and in ways hard to detect except retrospectively. Consider how factors promoting the development of Christianity would once have been hard to detect. Who from available evidence would have been able to say, at various points in the early years of Christianity's history, that ideas associated with an obscure prophet and a ragtag bunch of his followers would come to hold sway over the minds of billions? (Similar points could be made about the rise of science itself.) As David Wilson points out, when doing historical work we need to 'transpose' our minds in such a way that the future of historical figures – part of our past – loses the 'fixity and inevitability' we are inclined to see in it given how things in fact turned out, and instead takes on the uncertainty that it had for those historical figures (Wilson 2002, 23–4). If we do this, it will be easier to see how very differently things might have turned out – in the present case, religiously, if we take modern science out of various equations. Putting modern science back in, we can see that, with it there, all those other possibilities, threatening to monotheism, are going to find it more difficult to get themselves realized.

Other examples from the actual world, closer to the present, might be utilized here too. Cultural movements of the last few hundred years show how subtly varying understandings of the divine in nature can develop even in the midst of a monotheistic culture. Some of these movements might have flourished much more conspicuously than in fact they have done and blossomed into serious religious competitors for monotheism in the absence of science and its cultural effects. Take Romanticism. Perhaps Romantic pantheistic tendencies, which remained fairly close to monotheism, would in the absence of science have drifted towards polytheism. In this connection it is instructive to note that Romanticism was in fact halted in part by a realism and naturalism that betrayed the influence of science (Stromberg 1968, x–xii).

Even more recently, forms of religion veering away from monotheism and also away from a scientifically determined picture of the world, such as new age religion or paganism, have had a cultural impact, but an impact sharply restricted – at any rate so far – in its demographic consequences. The cultural status of science could very well have something to do with this, among other factors. Even though, as the sociologist Steve Bruce points out, scientifically sophisticated moderns can believe very strange things (Bruce 2006, 37), the 'strange things' offered up by new age religion and paganism have not advanced beyond the periphery of our culture. Perhaps the power of our internalization of scientific concepts such as the concept of natural laws, an internalization that would tend to resist believing that the activity of gods or goddesses is evident in natural cycles or that spiritual energies are to be found in physical objects, is underestimated by those who would deny science a role here. Bruce, as it happens, provides statistics to support the view that the 'demand' for new age products in Britain is very small, against fellow sociologists such as Linda Woodhead who think new age religion is making serious inroads in Britain and elsewhere (Bruce 2006, 40–2). Woodhead, for her part, appears in a recent piece (Woodhead 2016) to have somewhat moderated her earlier view that the West is on the brink of a 'spiritual revolution' involving new age religion (Heelas and Woodhead 2005). Almost in passing she notes, while characterizing the changing of religious norms, that 'the idea of "creation" has been supplanted' by ideas from physics and that human life is seen as governed by 'naturalistic evolutionary' processes; these are, she adds, 'views which simply need not be defended these days' (Woodhead 2016, 259).

Perhaps, then, the bulwark of science has had some work to do after all. Monotheists who survey the history of Europe and of the wider West have reason to be grateful that it was there.

3 Is Science Taking Over Monotheism's Traditional Roles?

We have seen that for a considerable period of time, the rise of science supported monotheism by adding to its arguments and by helping to prevent its main rivals from becoming live options, culturally speaking. Even today, most people would say that if any theistic view is true, it is monotheistic. An internalization of the notion of universal laws of nature has made explanation of natural events by reference to the decisions of gods – and more generally the notion of fundamental divisions and discontinuities in nature – seem less intuitively plausible to pretty much everyone in the West.

But monotheism can be regarded as the *most* plausible theistic option without being viewed as *overall* plausible or worthy of belief. A good deal of time has passed since the heyday of natural theology, and there have been many further cultural developments. The early rise of science led to ever more dazzling scientific performances as the nineteenth century turned into the twentieth and the twentieth into the twenty-first. Meanwhile, monotheism's cultural standing has diminished – the many well-known successes of secularism are a testament to that. This ancient view has been set back on its heels. And science is widely viewed as having had a good deal to do with this. Fairly soon, some think, science will put the monotheistic God, along with all other gods, in the rear-view mirror for good.

Much has been said about this perspective. Recently, a lot of it has been negative and disparaging. Charles Taylor, for example, in various places (e.g. Taylor 2007, 4) suggests that the narrative just mentioned about science's cultural power greatly oversimplifies and distorts actual historical processes. What I want to investigate is a particular way of giving a clear shape to the narrative and attempting to make it plausible – a useful way of understanding the challenge posed by science, fully risen, to the cultural status of monotheism. On this way of thinking, monotheism today is in danger of disappearing into the background (perhaps for all practical purposes it has already disappeared) as science *takes over the roles* that monotheism once filled for us. What I particularly have in mind is an explanatory role, which concerns the provision of an intellectually satisfying understanding of the world, and an existential role, which has to do with the procurement of meaning and fulfilment in our lives. If science were to take over, culturally speaking, in these departments, which are of course linked, then even if there remained sizeable pockets of monotheistic belief – indeed, even if those beliefs were true – monotheism's cultural raison d'être would be lost and its cultural standing would collapse or be severely diminished. Monotheism would, in centrally important respects, have been made culturally redundant.

But *is* it happening? To see whether it is, we will need to steer clear of the exaggerated claims of partisans in this discussion, both partisans of the view that monotheistic belief retains its cultural significance and partisans of the view that science has become the be all and end all, culturally speaking. We will also need to avoid inferring a descriptive conclusion from normative premises – a view about how monotheism is doing culturally from thoughts about its objective truth or reasonableness. Of course, something that matters to partisans may also matter to us, depending on its actual or likely cultural influence. And the arguments that can be discerned by thinking normatively here need not be irrelevant for us either. It's just that it is their actual effect or likely effect going forward on human cultural development that matters in the present context rather than their reasonableness or soundness per se.

3.1 The Explanatory Role

I begin with the *explanatory* role that monotheism has traditionally filled in our culture. Here one is tempted to say that the view we are investigating is provided with a head-start by what we saw in the previous section. For monotheism's explanatory capacity must have already appeared somewhat limited or qualified to pretty much any culturally aware monotheist in the last few centuries simply because of the agreed power of science to explain, in principle, virtually all happenings in the natural world!

Take a late nineteenth-century monotheist who has accepted Darwinism. They still conceive God as creator and, at least broadly speaking, designer; presumably God is the initiator of evolutionary processes. But because what God created and designed – an orderly, lawlike universe – has allowed science, including evolutionary science with its many discoveries about human life, to come into its own, our monotheist is now feeling the effects. As suggested, the existence of a monotheistic deity will still be posited to explain the fact that there *is* a universe and that it is ordered in a manner allowing science to succeed. Thus God is held to appear, somewhat dimly, further back in the causal chain even for ordinary events explained by science. But in relation to the most pressing explanatory questions about goings-on in nature, including now many questions about the human body and human relationships, monotheism must seem explanatorily redundant even to our monotheist. What humans most needed to learn about infectious diseases, for example, were facts about germs, even if the existence of God lies behind both germs and disease. And science taught us about germs. Our monotheist knows this. And the more science reveals, and the more sophisticated and exquisitely precise and accurate its explanations, the more science has to loom, psychologically, whenever the notion of explanation is broached, even for them. A more persuasive case for specifically monotheistic explanatory significance could perhaps be made, by our late nineteenth-century monotheist, in relation to occasional special events, some of them experiences, that appear to involve contraventions of the laws of nature – miracles. But these latter events are precisely regarded as occasional, and indeed they are generally held to be exceedingly rare, even by monotheists, once science gains its hold on European minds.

So what would it take for science to go all the way – to make monotheism appear truly and completely redundant in matters of explanation for us today? What should we expect to see? It may seem that despite science's precision and accuracy on matters close to home, this could never occur since, even ignoring apparent miracles, we can never explain the very existence of the universe or its most general regularities in scientific terms, and pretty much every cultural observer is aware of this. But here it is important to notice that science can take over monotheism's explanatory role even while not performing it just as monotheism did. The role, culturally speaking, is to explain everything humans want to have explained. Thus science could come to seem explanatorily suffi-cient, not by providing some purely natural explanation of nature, which will appear impossible, but by bringing it about that we *stop wanting* any such thing. The entire focus of humans could shift to the realm where science has been so successful, the realm of nature. Is there any reason to see this as occurring?

Certainly among many intellectuals and academics in our universities, it appears to be occurring. In a famous 1948 BBC radio debate between philosophers Bertrand Russell and Frederick C. Copleston, the former responded to the latter's claim that the cosmos requires explanation with an oft-cited line: 'I should say that the universe is just there, and that's all'. This view, that the existence of the universe is a brute fact – a fact lacking an explanation but needing none – is widely held among intellectuals and academics today, who overwhelmingly favour science when it comes to understanding the world. As for philosophers specifically: a recent survey has it that 73 per cent deny the existence of God (Bourget and Chalmers 2014). Have these philosophers substituted for monotheistic belief some other form of religious belief? No, the vast majority accept *scientific naturalism*, the view that nature, explored and progressively revealed to us by science, is all there is – Russell's view. Their view is a simpler one than monotheism. Instead of a single deity, who creates a universe, it posits a single reality; God is subtracted and only the universe remains. This view allows science, at least in principle, to explain everything. Although scientific naturalists can offer no explanation of the very existence of nature in non-natural terms, they feel no inclination to do so. No such explanation is needed, they will tell you. And for the explanations that are needed, we should look to science (Rosenberg 2012).

The one area where scientific naturalists sometimes feel a little vulnerable and can be made to appear defensive involves the explanation of consciousness. The so-called hard problem of consciousness – the problem, roughly, of why what the physical brain does should be accompanied by subjective experiential states; why there should be 'something it is like from the inside' to be in this or that brain state – is especially vexing. People certainly want *this* problem to be solved and for consciousness to be explained, but it does not appear that these results will be achieved anytime soon.

In response, some thinkers have insisted, as scientific naturalists must do, that science as we understand it will eventually enable a solution of the problem, if it has not already done so (Searle 2004). Others think we need to make use of available ideas that stretch or break the bounds of current science – ideas like panpsychism, which tries to solve the problem by making consciousness a fundamental part of nature, in some way and in some measure present everywhere in it (Goff 2019). Still others say we should be open to the possibility of brand new ideas of this sort emerging in the future (Nagel 2012). But it is highly significant that when it comes to the fundamental character of reality, even those in the latter categories are naturalists, holding that nature is all there is. They simply have less confidence in the notion that science as we today understand it will be able to reveal all of it to us. Moreover, they do not deny that a successful explanation of consciousness would in *some* way be continuous with the effort to understand the natural world represented by current science. Consider Goff's subtitle: *Foundations for a New Science of Consciousness.* Meanwhile, thinkers influenced by monotheism and willing to defend a dualist response to the problem of consciousness – for example, Swinburne (2013) – appear in relatively small pockets of academia these days and find themselves not taken very seriously by the majority. Thus, on balance, even when the problem of consciousness is brought into our account, the perspective from academia is very largely on side, broadly speaking, with science and opposed to monotheism and associated non-naturalistic ideas when it comes to providing explanations of things.

Now, intellectuals and academics often exert a cultural influence that is out of proportion to their numbers. And sometimes, as with pioneering work that has technological applications, their ideas signal where the culture is going even if it's not there yet. But within the larger population they are usually in the minority, in terms of numbers. So even if *they* would mostly hold that science is making monotheism explanatorily redundant, it is possible that things in the culture overall are different – more mixed, perhaps, and less science-centred as well as less obviously moving in that direction.

Perhaps it will seem, in line with what I said about our late nineteenth-century monotheist earlier, that people in general *must* tend to be similarly science-centred because we have all absorbed the explanatory power of science and rely on it continually, for example when thinking about how to deal with medical problems or in our constant employment of technological spinoffs from science such as the iPhone. Moreover, we are continually hearing about science-related exploits in the news. But, as we noted earlier, referencing the sociologist Bruce, humans are notoriously capable of inconsistency in belief and action. David Martin, similarly, speaks of 'the manifold character of mental space', in which 'many different modes of ideation and discourse can be entertained simultaneously and selectively drawn upon according to context' (Martin 2011, 125). We humans can praise science one day and ignore it the next when considering how to explain some 'spooky' happening in our vicinity. And of course monotheistic religion – whether Jewish, Christian, Islamic, or other – with its distinctive account of larger cosmological facts has not exactly gone by the wayside. Perhaps even what we said about the late nineteenth-century Darwinian monotheist needs to be in some way qualified to take account of all this properly. I propose that we now broaden our inquiry, considering some of these other cultural facts more closely, to see how well a broadly naturalistic explanatory perspective, linked to science, is doing in the culture as a whole.

One such fact, a fact that should make us less ready to think of the culture as a whole as shifting in a naturalistic direction, comes to us, ironically, from science itself – in particular, from the cognitive science of religion (CSR). CSR is a young field of study, but here is a clear fact about the evidence it has so far amassed and assessed: it strongly suggests that we humans have evolved a religious bent, and even more specifically, have evolved a tendency to favour agential religious ideas – ideas involving the notion of *personal agency* of the sort exercised by the monotheistic deity as usually construed (Atran 2002; Barrett 2004; Boyer 2002; Guthrie 1995; Slone and McCorkle 2019).

Now, supernatural agents, of course, are conceived as *doing* things. So what CSR suggests is that however much we are influenced by science – and even if inconsistently – humans may be expected to take ideas like the monotheistic idea of a personal God seriously and often look to them for an explanation of goings-on in the world around them or for the very existence of the world. According to a central concept of the field, our tendency to do this kind of thing betrays the operation of an evolved mental tool that Justin Barrett calls the 'hypersensitive agency detection device' (HADD), which sponsors a survival-conducive tendency – exercised, quite literally, just to be safe – to form the belief that agents, including supernatural ones, are present in situations where the evidence is ambiguous (Barrett 2004, 31–44). Perhaps this helps to explain why even educated humans (for whom a knowledge of science will help to make the overall available evidence *at least* ambiguous) may sometimes still feel a desire to attribute strange or beneficial or – at the cosmological level – mysterious happenings to God. Barrett goes so far as to argue that a naturalistic atheism is 'relatively unnatural and, unsurprisingly, a very uncommon world-view' (Barrett 2004, 108). People who are not intellectuals and academics, which is to say most people, do not work 'in an environment especially designed to short-circuit intuitive judgments tied to natural day-to-day demands and experiences', and so should be expected not to share the naturalistic worldview (Barrett 2004, 118).

There are ways of checking and possibly confirming whether this is true. One of these involves survey data. (The internet sources to which most of the following remarks – as well as some that come later – are indebted are cited in my Bibliography at the end of this Element.) According to surveys done by the Pew Research Center, there are many more believers in God or some higher power in America than in western Europe, but even in the latter domain they make up the majority in the general population. In America as a whole, apparently, the percentage of believers is larger than the percentage of atheists in philosophy mentioned before. Indeed – and this result is directly relevant to our question – around half of American adults go so far as to agree that God *determines* what happens to them all or most of the time. Now, America is of course often regarded as an outlier in these respects, and it is interesting to note that for specific countries in Europe, such as Sweden and Denmark, the numbers are often different than they are for the general population, with declared believers decidedly in the minority. But we nonetheless have support for the robust survival of the notion of God-as-explainer in various parts of the West, however inconsistent that notion may be with what many adults also believe about science. Apparently, many people today would still feel that something important had been lost – would feel intellectually dissatisfied – if they were forced never to explain events, special or mundane, local or cosmological, by reference to the hand of God.

In the face of such evidence, naturalists will sometimes point to the rapidly growing number of nones – those who respond to questions about religious affiliation with 'none' – mentioned by recent surveys. According to the 2018 biennial figures from the General Social Survey (GSS), a long-running measure of religion in America, the number of nones, which has been growing steadily, is now as large as the number of those who identify as evangelical or Catholic – each of these three groups in 2018 made up around 23 per cent of the American population. But it would be a big mistake to infer that at least 23 per cent of Americans are now scientific naturalists. Many nones still believe in God or a higher power and so count as monotheists: in America, believers are indeed in the majority among nones, though in western Europe they are not. Those most likely to be naturalists, who think there is *nothing* more, are the nones who self-identify as atheists (usually this means they are naturalistic atheists), and atheists, as Barrett's reasoning would lead one to expect, continue to make up a relatively small proportion – varying from one country to another – of the nones and a *very* small proportion of the general population. In America this is less than 5 per cent. According to the surveys undertaken by the sociologist Linda Woodhead, something similar is true of the UK:

> Only 13 per cent of nones are secular in this strong sense – which amounts to under 5 per cent of the population. So the growth of 'no religion' cannot be conflated with the growth of the secularism championed by the 'new atheists'. Indeed, atheism has not been growing anything like as fast as 'no religion', and atheism does not share the youthful age profile of 'no religion'. (Woodhead 2016, 250)

Survey data therefore provides some confirmation for what the first CSR results are suggesting, and in any case shows that scientific naturalism is not nearly as potent in the culture at large as it is among many intellectuals and academics. Can scientific naturalists nonetheless claim that the rise of science is an important factor in such *reductions* in monotheistic belief as the surveys show, and that *eventually* science will come to govern all our thinking about the explanations of things? Two issues need to be distinguished here. One is whether science is actively contributing to the loss of monotheistic belief, and the other is whether it is doing so in a way that should lead us to expect the mentioned result with respect to our explanatory proclivities. The answer to the second question could be 'no' even if the answer to the first is 'yes'. And apparently it *is* 'no'. This is explained by the fact that the proper answer to the first question appears to be at most a qualified 'yes'. Let me explain.

As it happens, a number of different causal factors are involved in the diminishment of monotheistic belief, and they involve science only indirectly and irrelevantly. Even Bruce, who defends the minority view that the West is on its way to complete secularization, and thus regards monotheism as on the way out, culturally speaking, does not place science at the centre of his proposal. As he puts it:

> [T]he idea that science displaces religion in a zero-sum contest to explain the world is largely a red herring. Contrary to the expectation of liberal theologians and advocates of the 'higher criticism' in the 1890s, modern people seem quite capable of believing all sorts of twaddle (witness the popularity of alien abduction stories or theories of racial superiority). Insofar as science does impact faith, it is through technology (rightly or wrongly) giving us a sense that we are masters of our fate. Medieval peasants quite reasonably saw themselves as being of no significance in the eyes of either their worldly masters or their Creator God. Modern Western consumers think rather highly of themselves: they choose their microwaves, they choose their governments, and they choose which God to believe in and in what manner. (Bruce 2006, 37; cf. Bruce 2013, 43–5)

The central factors in secularization, according to Bruce, are 'egalitarianism, individualism, and diversity' (Bruce 2006, 37). He, in concert with other sociologists of religion, credits Peter Berger, who speaks of a 'market of world views, simultaneously in competition with each other' (Berger 1979, 213), with a vital insight. In an essay on science and secularization, the prominent sociologist of religion David Martin broadly agrees, while mentioning a number of other factors, including 'the impact of secular control of education and the media' and 'the displacement of religious solidarity by national solidarity or the claims of party political ideology'. His conclusion about science here is in line with Bruce's:

> [T]hese assorted ideas and influences ... clearly have little to do with the impact of science, apart from the indirect consequences of scientific invention.

> Science as a technical procedure, available in this context or in that, is not the
> same as science as a mode of understanding. (Martin 2011, 121)

On our two questions, then: yes, science arguably *is* actively contributing to the
loss of monotheistic belief, though only in the context of a number of other
perhaps more important factors; and no, it is *not* doing so in a manner that
should lead us to expect science to eventually govern all our thinking about
explanation. Things are more complicated than that, and where clarity about the
complications is achieved it reveals that science-related factors are mostly
propping up our sense of personal power and individual importance – thus
helping to enable what Charles Taylor calls 'the massive subjective turn of
modern culture' (Taylor 1991, 26) with its secularizing tendencies – rather than
marching us towards a future in which science alone will claim our attention
whenever something needs to be explained, and God is shut out.

The upshot is this. For some reason or combination of reasons, including
perhaps such as science itself, through CSR, is discerning, monotheism has not
in any thoroughgoing way been made redundant in our culture at the level of
explanation because of the rise of science, and nor is it clearly on the way to
becoming thus redundant. Monotheistic belief and the factors that sustain it are
evidently putting up some fairly strong resistance to any such result. And where
monotheistic belief is failing, various factors are involved that appear to include
science at most indirectly and often irrelevantly. Even if things are changing and
scientific modes of explanation are looming *larger*, explanatorily, in the culture
as a whole, there is no way to tell how far this will go. Perhaps it will at some
point go all the way. But it is equally possible that associated trends will
eventually reach a ceiling, well short of 'all the way', beyond which our evolved
nature and our cultural circumstances do not permit us to go.

3.2 The Existential Role

I turn now to the *existential* role that monotheism has traditionally filled for
people in the West and the question whether something in the rise of science is
successfully challenging monotheism's cultural status in this respect. It is clear,
from survey results, that fewer and fewer people are finding their existential
needs satisfied by monotheism-associated activities or experiences, though the
degree of distancing from monotheism varies from place to place. Especially
telling as indicators are the numbers for those who attend religious services
regularly and those to whom religion is very important, which in various parts of
the West are going down. But notice that such trends might well be caused by
something other than the rise of science. So we will have to be careful to treat as
separate issues whether monotheism is experiencing cultural diminishment on

the existential side of things, which appears indeed to be the case, and whether the rise of science is at the root of this.

Perhaps it will seem that if the rise of science has not done much to make people forget about God when explaining the world or things in the world, as we saw in the previous subsection, then we should expect a similar result when it comes to the displacement of monotheistic resources for the procurement of meaning and fulfilment in our lives. Now the two dimensions, explanatory and existential, are certainly connected. Although one might find the explanatory tendency without the existential result – the eighteenth-century English deists come to mind – it is hard to see how the converse is true: one could hardly experience the world as imbued with meaning and one's life as fulfilling because of the apparent truth of monotheistic ideas without taking them to be involved in the explanation of *something*, for one would then (at least implicitly) be viewing the activity of God as explaining one's *experience*. But this is only to say that the persistence of the explanatory tendency is a necessary condition for the continued experience of the existential result. If it is not also sufficient – and as the English deists suggest, it is not – then some other condition (or conditions) will also be necessary, and perhaps the rise of science will suffice to put a dent into *this* even if not into the persistence of monotheistic explanatory tendencies. Here is a candidate for such an additional necessary condition: that no *other alternative* source of meaning and fulfilment will be taking over from monotheism and its representatives in our culture. We should now consider whether the rise of science is successfully challenging monotheism's cultural status precisely by generating such an alternative.

What might the alternative be? Perhaps we ought to think of it as science itself, in its modern incarnation, especially in respect of its ability to generate excitement, inspiration, and awe (awe both in relation to technical wizardry and before nature, the object of science), as well as a sense of deep connectedness in nature, contentment with one's identity as a natural being, and hope for humanity's future. People who are affected thus by science often are, at least implicitly, scientific naturalists. But their overall existential orientation deserves another name. Let us call it *scientific humanism*. Consider here the sorts of attitude sponsored by, say, Richard Dawkins' many books about science or by BBC nature documentaries. Often, people who produce and consume such books or films will eat, sleep, and breathe science and the fascinating natural world it reveals. They revel in the latest discoveries and in every detail of the emerging scientific picture of our place in an evolutionary world. They feel a bracing exhilaration and deep reverence before the wondrous immensities of the universe. Though, like many others, sensing the dangers of climate change and indeed very familiar with the details of various existential threats, they may feel quite confident that human beings can and will, with the help of science, rise to the challenge of surviving into the future, even the deep future – perhaps by transplanting members of the species into other, non-terrestrial environments. Underlying everything is the calming sense that, as human, one *belongs* to the natural world, an endlessly fascinating larger reality that one is privileged to know as no other creature belonging to it ever has, the knowledge of which may powerfully transform in positive ways future chapters of humanity's story.

Many resonate with such thoughts. Science, for them, provides an anchor in the world, a meaning-filled source of identity. Sometimes such scientific humanism is even developed in a manner including new ways of being together with others, something analogous to church services, only with secular science and associated experiences and activities affording a focus. The jury is still out on how successful such secular forms of religion-like community will be (Hill 2019). As the psychologist Michael Price has observed, monotheistic and other forms of uncontroversially genuine religion have long made possible 'inter-generational communities who interact regularly and who share values and worldviews; networks of mutually supportive long-term relationships; opportunities for fellowship and social bonding; and ritual commemorations of life's most meaningful events' (Price 2015, n.p.). Religious notions of transcendence are hard to make up for in secular communities. In particular, Price notes the difficulty of duplicating religion's ability to appeal to all kinds of people, to make members feel they are part of a force for good in the world, and to project gravitas. Already, therefore, we see some of the difficulties faced by the attempt to replace what monotheism has offered, existentially speaking, with scientific humanism.

But quite apart from the issues highlighted by Price, we should ask ourselves this: who are these 'many' that I have said resonate with such an enterprise? They are obviously people who have the wherewithal to understand science and who think a lot about *it* instead of about other things. Thus they still make up a group with fairly special characteristics, much as we saw academics and intellectuals do in the previous section, instead of being representative of the general population. Is the idea that science is in the process of taking over culturally, at the existential level, perhaps a bit of wishful thinking on their part instead of a genuine reason for monotheists to be concerned?

As it happens, here too survey results can help us. The Pew Research Center addressed sources of meaning and fulfilment for the first time in 2017. Even in America, only 20 per cent of responses to an open-ended question on the topic mentioned spirituality and faith. Money, career, and family were mentioned more often, with family – at 69 per cent – mentioned most of all, and friends and activities and hobbies about as often. Moreover, responses to a forced-choice question cited family, being outdoors, spending time with friends, caring for pets, and listening to music as providing 'a great deal' of meaning and fulfilment more often than they did religious faith.

So we have some confirmation for the view that secular sources of meaning and fulfilment are in the ascendancy these days. At the same time, learning, which could be seen as related to science, was mentioned by only 11 per cent of Americans. In addition to religion and family, a variety of other options including career, money, friends, activities and hobbies, health, and home and surroundings were mentioned more often than learning in responses to the open-ended question. The popularity of being outdoors could also be linked to science, though the connection is not very clear; obviously many people, including hunters, hikers, climbers, etc., enjoy being outdoors who may know or care little about science. Here one might also note that only 5 per cent of Americans cited being outdoors as the *most* important source of meaning and fulfilment, as we might expect them to do were it linked in their minds to the sort of science-based identity described earlier.

These results therefore provide some confirmation for the notion that although science may have great value at the existential level for many, the many are not many enough or diverse enough to seriously threaten the value afforded by religion – which here of course is monotheistic religion. And although it might be tempting to suppose that science is responsible for the religion numbers being relatively *low* in both surveys, it would be more plausible to say that the competing popularity of any number of other things associated with family, career, money, friends, activities and hobbies, being outdoors, caring for pets, and listening to music is responsible. *Secular* is not the same as *scientific*.

Thus such evidence as we have does not support the view that scientific humanism offers an alternative source of meaning and fulfilment that is displacing monotheism. Perhaps things will be different in this respect in the future. But the contemporary success of a scientific challenge at this level is not borne out. However, there is another way in which the argument in favour of science might be developed here. Perhaps the rise of science does not directly generate an alternative source of meaning and fulfilment in the manner we have been considering, but rather has results that represent a sufficient condition for *other* ways of accessing meaning and fulfilment; *other* secular alternatives, such as those listed earlier, to displace or make gains on monotheistic sources. In particular, as economic circumstances improve, such things as family, career, money, friends, activities and hobbies, being outdoors, caring for pets, and listening to music might be expected to become more able to afford meaning and fulfilment that competes with what is obtainable from religion. If so, and if science can take credit for improving our economic circumstances, then there may be reason to claim that science is still *indirectly* and at least in a loose sense 'taking over' monotheism's traditional existential role.

This may seem to bring us close to the idea that religion causally depends on *existential insecurity*, so that as nations become more economically and thus more existentially secure – 'existential' is here taken in a narrow sense that for all practical purposes could often be replaced by 'economic' – they become less religious (Norris and Inglehart 2004; Barber 2012). But the point I am suggesting does not depend on this view about the causes of religion. Even if the causes of religion are much more complicated and multifarious than this view suggests, and even if certain aspects or forms of religion will never disappear, monotheism's traditional existential function – in our sense of 'existential' – might still be challenged in the West by secular forms of meaning and fulfilment in the way we have seen it to be challenged. And science might still be enabling the challenge by improving our economic circumstances. Is this what is happening?

That economic circumstances have improved in the West can hardly be denied. Let us also grant that this is making it possible for monotheism's existential power to be marginalized, relatively speaking, by such other sources of meaning and fulfilment as were mentioned before, at least at present. Should we also accept that science is responsible for the improvement of economic circumstances? Here the facts about technology that were declared irrelevant in the previous subsection come into their own, becoming highly relevant. For it may be argued that advances in technology are behind economic improvement, and that the rise of science is behind those technological advances.

Notice first how plausible it is to say that science is causally linked in the relevant way to technology. Indeed, technology is often defined simply as the practical application of scientific knowledge. Even when practical experience or solitary invention lies behind some technological development, science will get its hands on the wheel at later stages of refinement. Harvey Brooks has a useful summary of some of the many ways science is involved here:

> Science contributes to technology in at least six ways: (1) new knowledge which serves as a direct source of ideas for new technological possibilities; (2) source of tools and techniques for more efficient engineering design and a knowledge base for evaluation of feasibility of designs; (3) research instrumentation, laboratory techniques and analytical methods used in research that eventually find their way into design or industrial practices, often through intermediate disciplines; (4) practice of research as a source for development and assimilation of new human skills and capabilities eventually useful for technology; (5) creation of a knowledge base that becomes increasingly

important in the assessment of technology in terms of its wider social and environmental impacts; (6) [a] knowledge base that enables more efficient strategies of applied research, development, and refinement of new technologies. (Brooks 1994, 477)

Of course, as Brooks argues, there is causation in the other direction too, as technology makes it possible to do science better – think of microscopes. But the point remains. As science rises, technology does too. Learning, through science, how nature does things, we can refine old ways and learn new ways of doing things ourselves, in pursuit of a wide range of purposes, many of them concerned with the improvement of human life. This is technological development.

What about the other point? Can we also say that the technological development enabled by the rise of science is behind economic improvement? Certainly it is a big necessary condition. When people document the huge changes and improvements, economically, over the past few centuries, technology always has a starring role. Of course, it can be argued that there were other necessary conditions too – among them, industrialization and globalization and mass communication. But even as the set of factors widens, science and technology remain prominent because, often enough, they are also in complex ways involved in the operation of those other factors! How could we understand industrialization without the steam engine, globalization without air travel or the internet, or mass communication without the radio?

Nevertheless, because of the complex conditions and subtle interrelationships involved in economic development, it would be an oversimplification to say straight out that science is responsible for it, and thus responsible for the changes feeding the existential sidelining of monotheistic religion. Of course, we can still say that where science through technology *has* contributed to economic improvements of the relevant kind, it has contributed to this result. This may, however, seem to fall considerably short of the notion that science is 'taking over' monotheism's traditional existential function.

But there is another way of making the basic point here that seems capable of producing a stronger result. Instead of focusing narrowly on economic improvement, we can think of how science has contributed a *wide range* of improvements to human life that, between them, suffice to greatly enhance the quality of meaning and fulfilment obtainable in relation to such things as spending time with family, career, money, friends, activities and hobbies, being outdoors, caring for pets, and listening to music. Perhaps if we can get evidence for this claim, talk of a science-based 'takeover' will sound less histrionic and more plausible.

Such evidence is not hard to find. Plenty of it appears, for example, in a recent book by Steven Pinker (2018). After displaying our progress across the full terrain of human life relevant to our discussion here, Pinker declares that it is 'science' that has 'granted us the gifts of life, health, wealth, knowledge, and freedom documented in the chapters on progress'. As a particularly potent example, he draws our attention to the fact that 'scientific knowledge eradicated smallpox, a painful and disfiguring disease which killed 300 million people in the 20th century alone' (Pinker 2018, 386). But there are other representative examples. Take the use of 'methane and steam to pull nitrogen out of the air and turn it into fertilizer on an industrial scale' (Pinker 2018, 75). Or how about the fact that '[t]hanks to advances in know-how, an hour of labor can buy more food, health, education, clothing, building materials, and small necessities and luxuries than it used to' (Pinker 2018, 94). Similarly: 'A dollar today … buys far more betterment of life than a dollar yesterday. It buys things that didn't exist, like refrigeration, electricity, toilets, vaccinations, telephones, contraception, and air travel, and it transforms things that do exist, such as a party line patched by a switchboard operator to a smartphone with unlimited talk time' (Pinker 2018, 117). It is also worth noting that 'as utilities and appliances penetrated American households during the 20th century, the amount of life that people lost to housework – which, not surprisingly, people say is their least favorite way to spend their time – fell almost fourfold, from 58 hours a week in 1900 to 15.5 hours in 1911', and that 'human-made light allows us to take back the night for reading, moving about, seeing people's faces, and otherwise engaging with our surroundings' (Pinker 2018, 251, 253). In a chapter on quality of life peculiarly relevant to our topic, Pinker details how what people are doing with the extra time and money that science-fed technology supplies includes such 'constituents of a good life' as 'connecting with loved ones and friends, experiencing the richness of the natural and cultural worlds, and having access to the fruits of intellectual and artistic creativity' (Pinker 2018, 255).

It seems right, therefore, to say that although often overlooked, no doubt because operating indirectly, certain important effects of science's rise are having a big impact on the shift away from religious sources of meaning and fulfilment. Instead of speaking of the 'invisible hand' of unobservable market forces, we might speak of the 'hidden hand' of science at work all around us in the construction of conditions enabling secular sources of meaning and fulfilment to displace or make gains on religious ones. Here, then, we see one way in which science, fully risen, *does* challenge the cultural status of monotheism with some degree of force. Though the explanatory challenge fizzled out under the force of our scrutiny, the existential challenge, in a subtle form that is easy to miss, has proved more potent.

4 Will Science Help Monotheism Rise Again?

The future, being the future, naturally permits less confidence for claims concerning its trajectory than the past or present. Perhaps we will see non-religious sources of fulfilment, aided by science, going from strength to strength, with the old resonances associated with monotheism increasingly unexperienced by succeeding generations (or provided with another cultural home). But human beings might also find new ways to think about God and to express religious predilections. I write in the midst of the 2020 Covid-19 pandemic, when churches, synagogues, and mosques are all closed and we wait for science to save us. Perhaps it will. Who knows what the results of that would be? But humanity, being humanity, may also be moved by this crisis, or some future crisis or renaissance, to reconnect with religious ideas and symbols – monotheistic ideas and symbols among them. Again, who knows?

We are, then, working in the shadow of considerable ignorance as we turn from past and present to the future of the relationship between monotheism and the rise of science in our culture. But precisely because of this fact, it is important to envisage both kinds of possibility, both religion-unfriendly and religion-friendly possibilities, and to think well about how either might be realized, going forward. Here I want to develop a set of ideas – perhaps initially counterintuitive ideas – about the religion-friendly possibility of *monotheism's continuing evolution*. It is easy to assume that when we have passed beyond polytheism and henotheism and arrived at the idea of one supreme and universal God, no further conceptual expansion or historical development can be had. But careful discussion gives the lie to this assumption. Furthermore, science, as we will see, could conceivably play a vital role in generating an enhanced cultural standing for some conceptual descendant of current monotheistic ideas of God. Science, with its high status, could conceivably help monotheism to rise again. According to John Hedley Brooke: 'Such is the richness of the subject [of science and religion] that it is well to set aside one's preconceptions. There are surprises in store' (Brooke 1991, 5). This oft-repeated point about the richness and complexity of the relationship between religion and science, confirmed by our own discoveries in previous sections of this Element, at least should make us willing to consider the possibility of such a startling turn of future events.

In the present section I flesh out this possibility. I shall begin by explaining what I mean by monotheism's future evolution in connection with certain broader religious claims, such as the philosophically modest and religiously ecumenical idea known as *ultimism*, the claim that there is a triply (metaphysically, axiologically, and soteriologically) ultimate reality. Ultimism arguably inherits most of monotheism's characteristics while being less vulnerable to cultural supersession than the understandings of God dominating religious discussion today. Then, in a series of steps, I will consider how science could contribute to the cultural success of this idea, or of some similar idea, in humanity's future. Here we will see how when more of us have internalized science's neglected results involving deep time and have come to think of religion in evolutionary terms, a new sense of human religious immaturity could come to prevail over other critical attitudes towards religion, and could also help to change the direction of religious behaviour, with good results for the cultural cachet of the new monotheism. Tending in the same direction, especially in a context of recognized religious immaturity, could be a widening awareness of the strangeness of nature's depths, as modern science conceives them, along with the influence of attitudes such as caution and humility as scientifically displayed.

There is no space here for a detailed discussion of all these ideas. But I hope they will provoke others to discuss various facets of the possibility in question, which I believe they do bring into view, more fully and adequately.

4.1 Can Monotheism Evolve?

The term 'evolution' itself has a scientific ring. Of course, in the present context, we are focused on cultural not biological evolution, but human sensitivity to the former has been greatly increased by our awareness of the latter. Today, indeed, possible relations and links between the two are more and more commonly discussed (see, e.g., Laland 2017; Lewens 2017; Richerson and Boyd 2006). No consensus or near-consensus on that topic which might be usable in the present discussion has yet emerged, but even so, we can see how the rise of science has had a role in making our present discussion seem salient.

The sort of cultural evolution I have in mind has two aspects: conceptual and historical. We will be thinking both about how the concept of God could evolve and about how some new conceptual product of philosophical thought about God could experience cultural uptake, swiftly or gradually becoming absorbed into the thought and behaviour of all or most of us and replacing previous ways of thinking about God. (Much of the latter discussion will occur in the following subsections.) Since such developments could not result in a high cultural standing for monotheism without the attainment, for this conceptual product and the corresponding claim, of wide influence and prestige, we should conceive of cultural uptake in a manner that affords it this implication. Fortunately, we will be able to do so and to make use of this notion for present purposes without being required to specify just how (causally speaking) and precisely in what ways we should expect the high standing of the new monotheism to be realized, if ever it is.

Let's begin with the conceptual side of things. And here an objection immediately presents itself. If our thinking develops in the way I've described, won't we simply generate some quite different religious conception which follows monotheism in the way that monotheism, conceptually, follows polytheism and henotheism, rather than a new version of monotheism? Not necessarily. Indeed, here we should acknowledge the particle of truth in the notion (mentioned earlier) that monotheism represents the end of a progression: having moved from many to few to *one*, there is in a pretty clear sense no further to go, if you want an affirmative religious proposition. So no additional change of the sort we had when 'one god' replaced 'many gods' can be expected. But there are still different ways of conceiving the one, and so long as not just unity (oneness) but also the themes of universality and ultimacy are respected and in some way incorporated as we reconceptualize (here recall what was said in Section 1 about the importance of these themes to an understanding of what makes monotheism distinctive), there will be no reason to regard the resulting concept as non-monotheistic or to withhold the label *monotheism* from the corresponding claim. Even if we should decide to speak of monotheism 2.0, monotheism 3.0, and so on (or in some functionally equivalent way), we will still have monotheism.

But don't the themes of universality and ultimacy themselves ensure that no further conceptual expansion is possible? Universality means that the religious significance of monotheism extends to everyone – and 'everyone' certainly appears unsurpassable! Ultimacy too seems unsurpassable by suggesting the very deepest, greatest, or most important.

This objection invites a similar response to the one I gave earlier for the other objection: monotheism as we know it today involves far more than just these themes, conjoined to the idea of divine unity. We have far more conceptual content. And so there is always the possibility of replacing this with different content. Consider the difference between omnitheistic and pantheistic content. The familiar omnitheism represents a person-centred way of thinking about one universal and ultimate reality. God on this view is a person-like being with omni-attributes: omnipotence, omniscience, and omnibenevolence. The less popular pantheism is decidedly not a person-centred view. Nonetheless, it is still a way of thinking about one universal and ultimate reality – a way that has all of reality in view. Even though monotheism today is viewed in a metaphysically dualist way, with omnitheism a familiar result of making this conception precise, we might one day, because of unforeseeable cultural changes, find a monist view such as pantheism in the ascendancy. If this occurred, what reason would we have to deny that monotheism had evolved through the erasure of the line between world and

God? Indeed, it could then be maintained that 'one' and 'universal' and 'ultimate' were being applied in an improved manner by the new conception, which, after all, makes God the *only* reality, a reality embracing all.

Another possibility, however, is easily overlooked here. This would involve a more subtle change, one suggested at the beginning of the previous paragraph: humanity might end up deciding that the notion of one universal and ultimate reality is sufficient *on its own*, without the familiar content of omnitheism or that of *any* other more detailed religious idea (including pantheism). This is the sort of possibility I want to focus on. What exactly would it involve at the conceptual level?

There is in fact some room for variation here, but what the various ways of realizing this possibility have in common is that all are broader or thinner conceptions of the divine than the notions central to omnitheism or pantheism. The relation between them and notions with more detail, such as omnitheistic and pantheistic conceptions, is this: the latter include the former but the former do not include the latter. So take our paradigm here – the idea of one universal and ultimate divine reality. An omnitheistic deity would fit this description, but we can conceive of a universal and ultimate divine reality that is not an omnitheistic deity. The same point, with appropriate substitutions, can be made about the notion of a pantheistic divine reality, and indeed about quite a number of specific detailed conceptions of divinity. Saying less, a religious claim involving the broader or thinner conception is compatible with more, though committed to nothing apart from what is in the core notion that defines it.

Of course, monotheism as we see it in the West today is hardly of the thin variety! Even if we shed the diversifying details of Judaism, Christianity, and Islam, we are left with a good deal of content, perhaps most familiarly represented by the philosophical omnitheism. So were we to shift from what one finds said about such matters today to the sort of view I've described, we would indeed have a shift, a change. Thus we could call it evolution. It would be evolution not because entirely new conceptual content had been introduced – the old monotheism will entail the new – but because a fair bit of conceptual content had been taken away. It would, we might say, be *evolution by subtraction*.

As I have said, there are various possible results of such subtraction. This is because even when understood to be relatively generic and left that way, terms like 'ultimate' and 'universal' are hardly precise. I will now make a case for one way of precisifying the relevant notions, which results in a form of the new monotheism I have called ultimism. Ultimism is, of course, a claim, not a conception, but we can identify the conception of the divine that makes it the claim it is. This conception is centred entirely on the notion of ultimacy, which gives it an underlying simplicity, but in it three kinds of ultimacy are combined, which gives it a richness not seen in the sort of vague reference to 'ultimate reality' common in religious studies contexts. Relatively thin our evolved concept may be, but it need not be skeletal.

A comparison with the old monotheism will serve to bring these three kinds of ultimacy into focus. For monotheism as we have known it, the existence of God the creator is the fundamental fact, in terms of which everything else concretely real must be explained. God is *metaphysically ultimate.* Now imagine someone saying only that there is a metaphysically ultimate reality, without the detailed content about a personal creator that the old monotheism adds to fill this out. What you have imagined is the first of the three things ultimism says, and the first kind of ultimacy.

According to the old monotheism, the inherent value of the divine is inconceivably great; the combined impact of God's infinite power and knowledge and love, for one who properly apprehends it, is such as to produce a response of worship. God, in other words, is *axiologically ultimate.* Now imagine someone saying only that there is an axiologically ultimate reality, without the detailed content about a personal power who knows and loves added to fill this out. What you have imagined is the second of the three things ultimism says, and the second kind of ultimacy.

But more is required to have a religious proposition. This 'more' could be seen as the 'other side' of axiological ultimacy: not now the ultimate inherent value of the divine, but its ultimate value for creatures and the world. I call this *soteriological ultimacy.* Monotheists have thought they saw it when they thought they saw God acting not as creator but as redeemer – acting in the world so as to ensure its ultimate felicity and that of all who come to know God – an action universally relevant whose benefits are universally available. But now imagine someone saying only that there is a soteriologically ultimate reality, without affirming the detailed content about a personal power who knows and loves and redeems which the old monotheism adds to fill this out. What you have imagined is the third of the three things ultimism says, and the third kind of ultimacy.

Ultimism, true to its name, says there is a triply ultimate reality. And that's *all* it says. What it has in view is more Plato's Good than Aristotle's Mover. One might of course give ultimism an omnitheistic or pantheistic filling, but ultimism per se does not require that either omnitheism or pantheism be true. There are other ways of elaborating ultimism too: given the variations found in these traditions, there could be Hindu, Buddhist, and Taoist elaborations of ultimism. Indeed, there may be many possible elaborations of it, including ones we've never thought of. And of course if ultimism is true, then one or another possible elaboration of it – perhaps one quite different from any we know or even one, superlatively rich, that is quite inaccessible to us – will be true too. But here we are imagining a conception in which no one such elaboration is included. Of course, by refusing to fill out our conception with the details of any single elaboration, we are in a very important way making room for *all* elaborations to be included, *disjunctively*. (A disjunction, in specifying what's true, says it is this *or* this *or* this, and so on – in the present case for a very long time!) All these disjuncts are, as it were, allowed to swirl instead of any one being selected. Ultimism says that *some*thing makes for metaphysical ultimacy and *some*thing for axiological ultimacy and *some*thing for soteriological ultimacy and *some*how these are united in one reality. But even with this indefiniteness and generality, we do not have insubstantiality. In particular, we are not leaving monotheism behind. Instead, we are gazing upon its golden core.

This golden core, with its idea of one reality in which metaphysical, axiological, and soteriological ultimacy are united, holds, I suggest, what is most important in the old monotheism. For what is God's love unless it saves us? And what is creation without foundational explanation? Moreover, when we see how triple ultimacy is independently affirmable – how the claim that there is such a reality can, as it were, be detached from the additional characteristics needed to generate the old monotheism – we may notice as well how in the shifting sands of cultural discussion, this sparer claim, ultimism, might preserve its salience and its prospects for future confirmation even if the old monotheism were to fall by the wayside. Saying less and compatible with more, there are fewer ways for any attack on it to succeed. Thus, in an age of secularism and scepticism, ultimism can certainly appear as a worthy successor to the more vulnerable and bulky claim that answers to the label *monotheism* today.

But that is only the conceptual side of things. What about the historical aspect of the cultural evolution I am asking us to imagine? However attractive ultimism may appear in the abstract, and to a philosopher, here we also need to imagine the evolved notion experiencing what I earlier called cultural uptake – becoming a mover and shaker in concrete historical terms. This would involve not just philosophical or even religious developments, but a corresponding shift in the focus and content of discussion about religion and God across a range of contexts, including those in which effective ways of opposing religion and belief in God are sought. And as we saw earlier, it would have to involve an overall increase in monotheism's influence and prestige.

Though we would clearly need more than philosophical discussion alone can deliver for all this to be realized, such discussion hardly becomes irrelevant at this point, and could indeed be the leading edge of change. Here prominent and popular critics of religion in the West might play a role. By learning about the conceptual evolution I have already described, they might come to see that the debunking of this or that elaborated ultimism – say, a fundamentalist Christian's idea of God – won't suffice to secure the intellectual credibility of scientific naturalism; ultimism plain and simple also opposes scientific naturalism. Since it is generally going to be more difficult to debunk ultimism plain and simple than to debunk some elaborated ultimism, the content and results of religion debates might change. And if people from various walks of life pricked up their ears as the new debate was carried on, the influence and prestige of the new monotheism could rise.

Of course, such developments would be greatly aided by a deeper openness to the evolution of monotheism and of religion more generally among critics, as well as by some evolved notion like ultimism experiencing uptake in a specifically *religious* manner. So long as most of the people making noise in the religious sphere are Christian or Islamic fundamentalists (or advocates of some other traditional view), the opponents of religion may feel little motivation to address a view like ultimism. This is where the proposal I am developing needs some extra help, and where, surprisingly, an appeal to factors available as a result of the rise of science begs to be introduced.

4.2 Evolution and Deep Time

We have seen how the usual articulations of monotheism – as well as of candidates to take their place – are relatively detailed and full of propositional content, and how by the simple expedient of subtracting content, monotheism could, at any rate conceptually speaking, be given new life. Now we will see how the point of proceeding in this way and also engaging the sparer view in a religious context could well become attractive to people in the West and in the rest of the world as, in decades to come, we all more fully absorb some of the best established results of science, namely those involving geological or 'deep' time and the broad evolutionary processes – both biological and cultural – that it holds. Our internalization of these results is not important here in itself or for its own sake, but rather because it may function as a stepping stone to awareness of human religious immaturity, as a result of which the nature of religious criticism may shift, and the potential of the new monotheism will be easier to see.

Let's begin by outlining the main scientific results involving time and change that I am saying more humans are likely to assimilate or to assimilate more fully in ensuing generations. These results come to us from the evolutionary sciences, which are teaching us to 'zoom out' to their vertiginous large-scale view, which, once we get things in focus, allows us to see our species in context. Scanning what science reveals of the deep past, we can detect innumerable changes to earthly environments, many extinction events, countless meandering pathways taken by natural selection with as many dead ends, and the quite contingent rise of mammals including apes, leading eventually to the various Homo species including our own, and finally to the dominance of *Homo sapiens*.

I say 'finally', reflecting the ease with which we treat ourselves as the end of things (in both senses of 'end'). Before the discovery of evolution, our species-based sense of importance was often sustained by the thought that we are made in the image of God or gods. But even after its discovery, we could (and did) think of ourselves as the most highly evolved, in a value-laden sense, and indeed as in some way the goal of evolution. Alfred Russel Wallace, co-discoverer with Darwin of evolution by natural selection, was comfortable speaking of 'all this glorious earth' which 'for untold millions of years has been slowly developing forms of life and beauty to culminate at last in man' (Wallace 1889, 476, 477). Michael Ruse reproduces a drawing of the tree of life by Darwin's German contemporary and promoter, Ernst Haeckel, which terminates with 'MAN' at the top (Ruse 2012, 108).

To counter such biased human propensities, it will be good to stay a little longer with what one sees when, seeking to be sensitive to science, one 'zooms out'. Here, where the consequences of deep geological time and planetary evolutionary processes are visible, we can see how human beings are one species of animal among others, evolving over hundreds of thousands of years, with potentially tens or hundreds of thousands to go. Our species is now around 250,000 years old. It is instructive to consider that even another 250,000 years would take us only halfway to the average lifespan of mammal species on our planet. And how many other species – whether organic or non-organic – will follow in the billion years or so that we are told remain for constructive activity on Earth?

Imagine a drawn timescale in which a 250,000-year period takes up 10 inches. This leaves exactly one-tenth of an inch for the past 2,500 years of cultural developments, which encompasses all that would normally be called science or philosophy in the West. As much time after as before the present for continuing cultural development would be radical in its potential results while clearly unremarkable within an evolutionary picture. A whole lot more time, for example the extra 750,000 years that would take us to the average lifespan of mammal species in another 30 inches or almost 3 feet, would be equally unremarkable. Even a great deal more time than that – and a lot more real estate! – would still leave us well within what science makes realistic (though of course not inevitable) for intelligence on our planet: a billion years would require 4,000 10-inch segments, which amount to 3,333 feet or about two-thirds of a mile. One needs to spend some time reflecting on that possible two-thirds of a mile against our one-tenth of an inch.

Doing so is a bit dizzying, so let's pull back a bit to think about religion, whose history is somewhat longer than the 2,500 years science and philosophy have had, perhaps more like 50,000 years. And let's contract the portion of deep time we have in view from a billion years to a period 1,000 times shorter, namely a million years, which as I've noted is how long, on average, mammal species on our planet endure. Then we can say that the whole history of human religion, which of course includes all that the Earth has ever seen of polytheism, henotheism, and monotheism, comes in the last fifth of the life of *Homo sapiens* (or the last 2 of 10 inches, if you're still thinking in those terms), and at the very beginning, in the first one-twentieth, of the enormously long period (40 inches, in all) that our species, if typical, will have had in which to undertake religious enquiries. Human religion, to use another image, is at a stage of development rather like that of a five-year-old who may live to be eighty. Of course, both religion and the five-year-old may die sooner, but if they do, they will die young.

I have elsewhere examined the factors that make it so difficult for us to get properly into view these facts about our place in time (see, e.g., Schellenberg 2014). But whatever the causes, one effect is clear: we have largely overlooked how short a time, in scientific terms, human religion has yet had and how long a period of further religious development the Earth might see. Even now, assimilation is slow: this is why I have said it may take some generations for human beings to internalize these facts. Might this particular awakening take much longer or be indefinitely delayed? Perhaps we can count on a fact at the heart of this Element – that the power of science in our culture is very great – for a negative answer to this question.

4.3 The Discovery of Religious Immaturity

Suppose then that before long, perhaps in a few generations, the human awakening to deep time and religion's youthfulness is much further along. This would make feasible such large shifts in thinking and behaving as my proposal about a new monotheism requires, because it would smooth the way for another realization: humanity is *religiously immature.*

That our species is religiously immature does not follow directly from the scientific truths about deep time and evolution I have just outlined. After all, the five-year-old might be a prodigy! But having attained the large-scale view afforded by science, humans will find it much easier to think in developmental terms and to imagine the religious dimension of human life as something that can change and grow over much time, that can progress or regress or stagnate. At that point, a new question will come into focus: what stage in this process have we reached? Unless human beings manage to clean up their act in a big way in just a few generations, the answer will be clear: we are still at an *early* stage of religious development. The five-year-old is not a prodigy.

Issues about large-scale species development are complex, but for a basic understanding of the concepts of developmental immaturity I want to apply here, it will suffice to make three points. First, we must distinguish between immaturity in the sense of *shortcoming* and immaturity in the sense of *potential* (Schellenberg 2019). To see the difference, notice how what you mean when you say of someone who is always carelessly getting drunk that they are 'so immature' differs from what you mean when you say of a first-time novelist that in respect of technique they are 'still immature'. Second, these two forms of immaturity are *connected* at least insofar as pervasive shortcomings can hold one back on the side of potential – can prevent one from making much progress along the developmental path towards one's potential. Our example works here too: someone constantly getting drunk won't get very far in the development of novel-writing skills. Third, we need to answer the question: potential for what? There are various possible answers, but in relevant cases, this will generally be the attainment of a *goal* of some kind, such as the goal of mastering the writing of novels.

Let's now apply these points to the religious dimension of the life of our species, with that self-congratulatory name *Homo sapiens*. A plausible goal here is this: either (a) discerning the existence and character of an ultimate divine reality or (b) discerning that no such thing exists or (c) discerning that humans are unable to reach as far, in their discoveries, as either (a) or (b). This is of course a rather ambitious goal for a humble earthly mammal species, and there are ever so many ways in which human shortcomings might prevent much progress towards it being made. And indeed, that last point reflects just how – so far – things have gone in the history of human work on religion. Here we need to recite to ourselves from the long list of developmental immaturities of shortcoming manifestly displayed by human religion of the past and the present. Think only of all the petty and (in the moral sense) small disagreements within religious communities, the vast ignorance of what is held precious by other religious communities, and the horrible violence that does not leak into the present from the past but flows freely. And I have not even mentioned our remarkable ability, full of ourselves as we are, to ignore how we *might be* religiously immature – how religious development might, for all we know, proceed at a pace better measured according to scientific timescales than human ones. The need to investigate a wide range of religious possibilities has hardly so much as crossed anyone's mind.

What about the irreligious – those who oppose religion? Here, at least in the present, there is much less violence, but there is still considerable ignorance of what is being rejected, and as great a lack of intellectual and spiritual empathy as the religious frequently display towards each other. Science is clung to as a saviour from the past, which in some respect it may well turn out to be. But in their enthusiasm for science, many have acquired the expectation that everything real can be reduced to the natural processes science is fitted to expose, rejecting religion both because it claims there is more to reality than this and because its most visible representatives often oppose scientific results. Moreover, nothing in their enthusiasm for science has led religion's opponents to the immaturity idea either. Even those fully aware of deep time who tout evolutionary ideas are, to their discredit, silent on the subject. Not surprisingly, here too religious investigation suffers.

If these admittedly potted characterizations seem to capture something familiar (for more detail see Schellenberg 2019), perhaps you will conclude with me that there are strong signs of religious developmental immaturity – specifically, of immaturity as shortcoming – both among those who favour religion and those who oppose it. Given the high ambition of the goal assigned to the religious dimension of human life, by reference to which our religion-related behaviour so far can be seen to be immature in this sense, much more would need to have been done in the past for us to now be very far along the path to that goal's attainment. And here the point about a connection between the two kinds of immaturity becomes applicable. Because of our vast religious shortcomings, we have not yet proceeded very far along the path towards that goal. And so we are religiously immature in both senses.

There is of course a positive side to this – a silver lining. Although our shortcomings look bad and should displease us, they also ensure that much more religious development may well be possible, especially if and as we rid ourselves of these shortcomings and put better behaviours and attitudes in their place. The species is presently religiously immature both in the sense of shortcoming and in the sense of potential. So, for all we know, a great deal more in the way of religious insight and discovery lies down the road, waiting for us to get our act together – waiting for us in our future. To revert to our example, if they stop getting drunk and go into recovery, our would-be novelist might yet achieve greatness in that domain!

All this, then, we may associate with the notion of human religious immaturity. All this, we are supposing, the human awakening to deep time and religion's youthfulness, sponsored by the rise of science, will soon allow more of us to bring into focus and take more seriously.

4.4 Some Effects of This Awakening

And that brings us to the next stage of this section's discussion, which is about the possible cultural effects of what has just been described. One effect we might expect is a change in how religion is criticized. In short, if religion's critics accept the immaturity thesis, then they will criticize religion as immature – the challenge to religion will be that it should grow up – rather than as defunct, hopeless, or superannuated. For to criticize it in the latter way instead of the former is to assume that the goal of development in the religious dimension of human life (specifically, either outcome (b) or outcome (c) from our earlier statement of that goal) has already been reached. And this assumption the immaturity thesis takes away.

How would such a change affect the prospects of a new monotheism, represented by a proposition like ultimism – the result of evolution by subtraction? I suggest it might well make many people, including many of religion's critics, much more open to such evolution and to efforts made on its basis, and much more willing to see it as part of a worthy attempt – for example, through investigation of a wide range of possible elaborations of the evolved monotheism – to promote further development and maturing in the religious dimension of human life. By the same token, religion's critics, or at any rate those holding to scientific naturalism, would realize that to make their case, this general proposition ultimism (or whatever general proposition the evolved monotheism turns out to be) must be shown to be false. And that job is going to be a lot more difficult than showing to be deeply problematic some religious fundamentalist's detailed belief. The upshot may well be, then, that through long discussion of this much more intellectually impressive proposition into which monotheism has evolved, the cultural status of monotheism – at least in those areas of the culture where intellectual discussion has its strongest effects – begins to rise. If during this time, as more creditable investigation occurs, new and interesting and plausible elaborations of ultimism emerge that no one had previously thought of, one can see how the cultural status of monotheism would be improved still further.

Here I need to issue a reminder that in this Element I am just trying to get an interesting but overlooked *possibility* into focus and make its possibility vividly clear. I am not claiming that this possibility will be realized or even that it should be realized. In this Element I am interested in the more fundamental 'could'. Everything I have been saying ought to be viewed in light of this relatively modest aim. But to achieve it, we will still have to do more. For we have so far said little about the sphere of religious activity per se, the practical sphere of praxis and ethics and spiritual pursuits, which has its own life apart from intellectual discussion and criticism, and would need to be affected appropriately in order for monotheism truly to rise again. How could this happen? Could that sphere be significantly affected at all, or is the foregoing discussion of ultimism just another version of the 'God of the philosophers', out of touch with and insensitive to the needs of concrete religious life?

A strong practical effect may seem difficult to imagine, especially when, as noted before, it appears that most of the people making noise in the religious sphere are conservative fundamentalists. Merlin Donald, who is at the forefront of mimesis theory, which emphasizes our strong evolved tendency to imitate each other, writes that this mimetic dimension of culture 'tends to be conformist and conservative, as seen in such things as religious ritual, royal coronations, and deep cultural habits such as ways of greeting, attitudes to authority, and so on' (Donald 2013, 190). Accordingly, change across the generations, including religious change, might be expected to occur slowly. But no one, including Donald, would say it is ruled out: 'A purely mimetic culture can evolve. Mimetic acts are expressive and thus inherently inventive and creative' (Donald 2013, 190).

In any case, here it is important to remind ourselves that because of *past* cultural evolution, the religious realm is already quite diversified, with some parts of it much more liberal than others. Non-conservative religion is already well represented – certainly well enough to permit it to grow significantly under the right circumstances. And to the liberalizing parts of religion, including their practical dimensions, we might expect the idea of religious immaturity to be quite attractive. As well as affording a new impetus and rationale for liberal attempts to make religion less violent, less sexist, and less dogmatic, it might fuel a range of new investigative endeavours, which could allow the new investigations lauded earlier to actually take place. Liberal religion, thus amended, could indeed now see itself as the cutting edge, with its talk of divine mystery viewed as prescient instead of escapist – a big and appealing change from present circumstances, in which liberal forms of religion are commonly viewed as being in the doldrums.

For such a reinvigorated religious liberalism, if it grew, a proposition like ultimism should provide an attractive central point of reference or framework idea. With the help of this idea, theological talk of mystery would be provided with clearer lines than it has now. Theologians today can sometimes seem to vacillate, claiming not to be atheistic but not clear on what they are. Critics are often inclined to jump all over theologians for appearing to hem and haw in this way. But given a deep awareness of religious immaturity, fed by large-scale science, and a new vision of monotheism conceived ultimistically, theology could explicitly embrace atheism, as usually conceived by its cousin philosophy, and move on, pointing out that only *personal* or *agential* ultimism has been left behind and that we all need to stretch our minds and hearts to see what more – and in particular what other elaborations of ultimism – the species has in it to discover and perhaps confirm as true. And even the idea that philosophical atheism requires personal conceptions of the ultimate to be left behind must be qualified. It is the idea that the ultimate is *exclusively* personal that has to be left behind, if traditional atheism is true. A rich elaboration of ultimism such as Spinoza's, for example, allows us to imagine a personal element as one among an infinite number of 'modes' of divinity (Schellenberg 2007, 52–3). Here the possibility to take note of involves addition rather than subtraction.

But in these references to liberal theology, are we again veering away from the practical side of things? Not at all. There is, after all, such a thing as practical theology. More generally, the intellectual and the practical are intertwined in religion. A quick way to see this is to notice how theologians have *communities*: they strain to provide an improved formulation for the ideas of a living religious community, to which they belong, and their ideas feed the ongoing experiments in living that religious communities represent. With this in mind, it becomes possible to imagine, at the limit, an awareness of human religious immaturity over time spurring the development of a global theology, with a common commitment, reflected in the life of religious communities, focused on the new monotheism or on 'God' in a correspondingly broader sense. At the same time, one can imagine a gradual convergence on details from only initially conflicting *positions* about what the details are – which now are circumspectly taken as such: that is, as positions only. In other words, belief in God might come to be restricted to the common centre, with various traditions coming to see their various more detailed views as representing what they are tasked with developing and defending and expressing existentially in a broad collaborative endeavour, one that might over much time lead to quite new detailed understandings transcending all of the old, even if not the stable centre. Some such arrangement is at least a reasonable aspiration for liberal theologians of the West, one that pioneering theologians today could work to realize. And it represents one clear way in which both practically and intellectually, monotheism could rise again.

Robert Wright, in his book *The Evolution of God*, envisages a possible future situation somewhat like this: 'Is it crazy to imagine a day when the Abrahamic faiths renounce not only their specific claims to specialness, but even the claim to specialness of the whole Abrahamic enterprise? Are such radical changes in God's character imaginable? Changes this radical have already happened, again and again. Another transformation would be nothing new' (Wright 2009, 442). But while Wright recognizes past changes and speaks of evolution, he is working without the benefit of an emphasis on our present immaturity. In its absence, he has recourse to the old idea of many existing religious paths somehow, despite their many contradictions, coming to be seen as leading to the same destination (Wright 2009, 442–3). With our religious immaturity recognized, however, we might instead and much more profitably entertain the thought that there will be many more possible depictions of the divine to work with in the whole history of humankind than are available in the twenty-first century! We might wish to preserve the golden core of all the ideas discovered so far while letting the latter go, or demoting them to a lesser status. And this could make all the difference.

In short, then, a new fund of ideas is made available by reflection on scientific ideas about deep time and evolution and the associated notion of human religious immaturity, which more and more people concerned with religion in the future may come to accept and live by: that human religious development has been held back; that we are consequently still at an early stage in the relevant developmental process; that it would be good for religion itself to evolve in ways that promote development; and that mono-theism and monotheistic religious communities in particular can evolve to help meet these needs. As we have seen, the new more modest monotheism we might expect to present itself in such circumstances, the product of evolution by subtraction, could find its cultural power significantly enhanced. If such occurred and the roots of this development were sunk in reflection on deep time and evolution, as here imagined, monotheists would have science to thank.

4.5 Strangeness and Humility in Science and Religion

But there is yet another way in which science might in the future help monotheism rise again. If evolution and deep time are, as it were, pushing from behind, then here we might think of science *pulling from the front*, as it marches into the brave new world of the future. Especially against the back-drop of a discovered immaturity in the religious realm of human life, the strangeness of respected scientific ideas in physics along with the attitudes of caution and humility that are familiarly associated with the work of science might play this vital role. For they might serve to enhance the possibility, and our consideration of the possibility, that the regions of religious reality, if populated at all, quite transcend our present capacities to grasp. They might furthermore permit religion to present itself more regularly and convincingly, in realms public and private alike, as dealing in profound mysteries rather than primitive superstitions. And the new monotheism, by responding to and codifying such thoughts and impressions, might plausibly be imagined to gain in respect and influence commensurately.

Wright remarks both on the strangeness of recent scientific thinking and the theological corollary some might draw here:

> In general, the quantum world – the world of subatomic reality – behaves in ways that don't make sense to minds like ours. Various aspects of quantum physics evince the property that the late physicist Heinz Pagels called quan-tum weirdness . . .. The bad news for the religiously inclined, then, is that maybe they should abandon hope of figuring out what God is. (If we can't conceive of an electron accurately, what are our chances of getting God right?) (Wright 2009, 446–7)

Again, we see human religious immaturity overlooked – otherwise, why the assumption that if we were going to get God right, we would have been able to do so by now? But more important for us at the moment is this notion that if the cutting edge in physics is so strange and mind-boggling, we might expect theological truths, if there are any, to be even more strange. Does this sort of move work?

It depends on how you formulate it. One might interpret the move this way: 'As we go deeper into the nature of physical reality, things get stranger (in the sense of more at odds with what makes sense to our hominin minds). So if we go even deeper, as we do when thinking about God, they could well be stranger still'. This formulation appears to make of God a deep – perhaps the deepest or most fundamental – *physical* reality. Wright, for one, sometimes seems comfortable with such a thought. But to think thus would mean betraying the new monotheism rather than defending it. Consider the content of ultimism in particular. Religious truths, if truths about a reality soteriologically and axiologically ultimate as well as metaphysically fundamental, would be of a different order from truths about the physical universe. An axiologically ultimate reality would transcend the physical universe – would be more than or other than the universe – rather than belonging to it, since the physical universe, be it ever so wonderful, is not *unsurpassably* great.

Yet even if all of this is correct, another formulation of the move Wright suggests is possible, and it may fare better, supporting rather than betraying the new monotheism as well as any sense, won from reflection on human religious immaturity, that we ought to be framing our religious thought in terms of it. Perhaps we might put it this way: 'As we go deeper into the nature of physical reality, things get stranger. So if we go even deeper, they could well be stranger still. And whatever is metaphysically *ultimate*, whatever is that (whether physical or transcendent of the physical) in terms of which all else – and so all these inconceivable things – is to be explained, could therefore be the strangest and most inconceivable of all'.

Notice that I've only had our strangeness argument conclude with a claim about what 'could' be the case. That is enough for present purposes, and a stronger claim would be poorly grounded in the available premises. For not only could it be that quantum physics will yield to some more humanly accessible physics in the future. It could also be that a person-like agent with an omniscient mind capable of understanding things far stranger than quantum phenomena has willed a world of things strange and familiar into existence. This is certainly what a defender of the old monotheism would say. And the basic features of persons and minds and agency are quite familiar to us, not strange at all. Perhaps they will seem to you to represent the most natural way of conceiving a divine reality.

But now recall religious immaturity. Recall also what we learned earlier in this Element, in connection with the cognitive science of religion, about the evolutionary appeal of agential religious conceptions, with which that natural-seeming thought of a person-like deity is clearly associated. And then think about the strangeness of quantum physics and the explanation afforded by the old monotheism once more against *that* backdrop. The possibility that the details of the old monotheism reflect limitation and bias and that we at present have no clue just how metaphysical ultimacy is instantiated, or just how axiological ultimacy is instantiated, or just how soteriological ultimacy is instantiated, even if there should be a metaphysically, axiologically, and soter-iologically ultimate reality, ought to appear enhanced – as more of a live possibility. This is what the strangeness of quantum physics, along with other counterintuitive complexities and subtleties of thought sponsored by the rise of science, can do to strengthen the appeal of the new monotheism, when pulling from the front.

It will be well to remember here that Newtonian physics, though of course ingenious and mathematically formidable, was much more accommodating to the human mind. It did much less than the physics of today to transgress human intuition. William Paley, as we have seen, could work comfortably within it in service of the old monotheism. A William Paley of the twenty-first century, with ambitions tempered by an awareness of religious immaturity, might continue to find support in nature for the notion, say, of divine unity, but he would be far more open to the possibility that the nature of the divine will be available to earthly minds, if ever it is, only when they have been stretched far beyond their present dimensions and capabilities by some combination of biological and cultural evolution. This would be nothing more than a rational response to the altered situation.

And it would be no more than the response that *humility* and *caution* can be seen to demand. These virtues, as well as others bound up with them, are the stock-in-trade of all good science. And although human beings are still rather often more cocky and arrogant and sure of themselves than they have any right to be, it is perhaps not too much to say that the rise of science has made the aforementioned virtues more respected among us than they once were – has increased *their* cultural cachet. Of course, we see boldness and independent-mindedness in such paragons of modern science as Darwin and Einstein, but humility and caution are there too, and indeed they form an indelible part of the image of such figures in the public imagination. Might this fact have its own contribution to make in support of ways of thinking and of being religious that feature the new monotheism, helping the science of the future to pull us forward, religiously speaking?

Imagine many William Paleys at work, exposing in detail the strangeness of science's results and moved by scientific caution and humility, all within the context of a recognized religious immaturity. There would be a greater boldness even if also greater conceptual modesty in the religious explanations they propose of the largest cosmological facts, and in their challenge to scientific naturalism. For the uncertainties sponsored by an awareness of religious immaturity are of a unique kind that at the same time justify openness to the thought that new religious insights with important metaphysical corollaries will appear in our future, and the need for such openness shows up a serious weakness in scientific naturalism – at any rate when the latter is put forward as confidently as it has been in recent years. The truth of ultimism in particular is incompatible with the truth of naturalism, so more openness to the former brings with it less assurance of the latter. Even a modern Darwin might be persuaded to show such openness when, in circumstances of the sort we are imagining, he is reminded of the virtues of caution and humility.

And what might come with such work by modest modern Paleys, or alongside it, in the culture of our future, given the simultaneous operation of the other factors we have been discussing? Here it is good to remember how a continually percolating interest in religious matters is predicted by the cognitive science of religion; this might now be allowed to erupt in new ways and take new forms. Perhaps we would see a greater excitement in the public at large about the prospect of larger religious goods and at the thought that it is in the context of such goods that the meaning and value of such undeniable goods as spending time with family, career, money, friends, activities and hobbies, being outdoors, caring for pets, and listening to music is best understood. Mystery can be stimulating when it reflects something more profound than intellectual escapism and is not intrinsically unrelievable, and both conditions are satisfied here for the mystery reinstated for religion by religious immaturity. Religious practice too might gradually be transformed, not least because the emphasis on caution and humility is not unfamiliar in the precincts of faith, and need only be reinforced and redirected by what has been learned from science.

I can imagine some doubts about the latter prospects based on the science-and-religion discussion we have today. This already appeals to the habits and virtues and results of modern science, but, as it happens, also features many defenders of the old monotheism. These individuals will often enough couch what they have to say in cautionary phrases about humility. Traditionalists on the basis of the influence of science may propose, for example, that we should be open to changing our minds about how traditional religious views are best formulated; that we should hold to treasured traditional views more tentatively or interpret old doctrines such as the impassibility of God or the providence of

God in new ways (Barbour 2000). But for some reason, they seem invariably to end up cautiously and humbly holding to traditional views! Other factors at work here – loyalty to a community, for example, or the conservative effects of mimesis (remember Donald's point from before) – have proved strong enough to prevent the valorizing of intellectual caution and humility from leading to anything like so big a change as would be represented by the new monotheism. Meanwhile, the existential challenge of science, as construed at the end of the previous section, grows stronger and the force of monotheism in the culture, much of which no longer feels the loyalties of the traditionalists, is weakened rather than rising again.

The points made here are well taken. And let me issue another reminder that I am not arguing that the new rise for monotheism I have described is certain to occur. Far from it. Perhaps it will fail to occur for reasons like those suggested here. What I have been trying to do is to get a new possibility into focus and to show how science could contribute to its realization, so that our set of options going forward is enlarged and so that we can see more clearly what we need to do if we want this one to be realized. Furthermore – and by the same token – the religious expressions of humility and caution I am interested in are *future* expressions, shaped by circumstances not our own. And I certainly do not imagine them doing the whole job by themselves. My point is that what we have seen of humility and caution in modern science and of their effects might in combination with all that we have already seen earlier on, including most recently the strangeness of ideas in physics, help a new monotheism to flourish and exercise influence in contexts both religious and non-religious. Pushed from behind by science and pulled from before, monotheism could just rise again.

5 Epilogue

When I started this Element on monotheism and the rise of science, I was not sure just how it would end. I had read enough to suspect how the historical part of the story would turn out. And I had my own work on related subjects – in particular a book on religion and science published the year before (Schellenberg 2019). At some point early in the process it struck me that an idea I have called ultimism or some idea like it could conceivably be a descendant in history – and a 'close continuer' – of the monotheism we have come to know and love (or hate). All in all, my sense was that claims about the challenges posed to religion and in particular monotheism by the rise of science were overblown. I thought I would do some investigating and see what new pieces of the puzzle might turn up if one thought the question through temporally, considering past, present, and future in succession. I wasn't sure how all the pieces would fit together.

Now things are clearer. Monotheism and science, as we have seen, were in various respects mutually supportive aspects of Western culture when the latter began its rise, a few hundred years ago, and also for some considerable time afterward. They were not enemies at all but rather friends. Science certainly is challenging monotheism today, or being used to challenge it, especially in intellectual circles. In the wider culture, however, the main explicit and direct forms of this challenge have made surprisingly little headway. If there is a serious, widely effective cultural challenge to monotheism emanating from science at all, it is more indirect: the 'hidden hand' of science clearing the way for other, secular sources of existential satisfaction to replace those associated with monotheism. And when we turn from past and present to the future, the picture changes again – or rather we see how it very well could change. Among the host of possible snapshots of Western culture in the year 2220 or 2320 are some that feature monotheism 2.0 doing quite well, culturally speaking, and doing well with – and even because of – the help of science.

Provocatively, then, we might put one of my concluding suggestions this way. When the total story of science's relationship to monotheism, past, present, and future, is told, even such tensions between science and religion as we see today could well appear somewhat anomalous – as moments of struggle bookended by periods in which cultural forces associated with science supported those allied with monotheism.

That word 'could' can be frustrating, signalling as it does the relative inaccessibility of the future. But it is also a sign of our freedom. To some extent, how the future will look – and in particular whether it will look anything like my provocative suggestion suggests it could – depends on *us*, on what we do today and tomorrow. Now perhaps you don't find anything appealing in the counter-intuitive notion of monotheism and science as friends. That's fine. Maybe you won't want to do anything to help promote a future in which they appear as friends. But those who do will be wondering how best to seek to realize such a goal. This Element contains some ideas.

These appear mainly in Section 4. But let me add one last thought – my other concluding suggestion. Whether science is able to fuel the resurrection of monotheism, whether that's how things turn out, depends not just on science but also on religion. In particular, it depends on whether, in monotheistic religion and thought of the *next* few hundred years, loyalty can be tempered by imagination and conviction by creative doubt.

To get to the second member of each of those two pairs, and to do it in religious contexts, may seem a big lift! But notice that I do not say that the first would have to be *traded* for the second. An important loyalty to religion, even to God, can continue among those who imagine a 'bigger God' and transformations of faith and practice suited to a continuing religious quest, a deeper religious maturing, on the part of our species. Likewise, conviction as to the truth of monotheism in some form need not be given up by those who entertain doubts about the adequacy of the details in its current depictions. Can we count on human religion to grow up in these ways? We cannot. But to apply Robert Wright (2009, 442) once more: 'Changes this radical have already happened, again and again. Another transformation would be nothing new'.

Bibliography

Atran, Scott. (2002) *In Gods We Trust: The Evolutionary Landscape of Religion*. New York: Oxford University Press.

Barber, Nigel. (2012) *Why Atheism Will Replace Religion: The Triumph of Earthly Pleasures Over Pie in the Sky*. E-book, available at: www.amazon .com/Atheism-Will-Replace-Religion-ebook/dp/B00886ZSJ6.

Barbour, Ian. (2000) *When Science Meets Religion*. London: SPCK Press.

Barrett, Justin L. (2004) *Why Would Anyone Believe in God?* Lanham, MD: AltaMira Press.

Barrow, John. (1988) *The World Within the World*. Oxford: Clarendon Press.

Berger, Peter L. (1979) *Facing Up to Modernity*. Hammondsport: Penguin.

Bourget, David and David J. Chalmers. (2014) 'What Do Philosophers Believe?' *Philosophical Studies* 170: 465–500.

Boyer, Pascal. (2002) *Religion Explained: The Evolutionary Origins of Religious Thought*. New York: Basic Books.

Brooke, John Hedley. (1991) *Science and Religion: Some Historical Perspectives*. Cambridge: Cambridge University Press.

Brooks, Harvey. (1994) 'The Relationship Between Science and Technology'. *Research Policy* 23: 477–86.

Bruce, Steve. (2006) 'Secularization and the Impotence of Individualized Religion'. *The Hedgehog Review* 8: 35–45.

Bruce, Steve. (2013) *Secularization: In Defence of an Unfashionable Theory*. Oxford: Oxford University Press.

Darwin, Charles. (1958) *The Autobiography of Charles Darwin*. London: Collins.

Davies, Paul. (1992) *The Mind of God: The Scientific Basis for a Rational World*. New York: Simon and Schuster.

Davis, Edward B. and Michael P. Winship. (2002) 'Early Modern Protestantism'. In Gary B. Ferngren, ed. *Science and Religion: A Historical Introduction*, 117–129. London: Johns Hopkins University Press.

Debray, Régis. (2004) *God: An Itinerary*. London: Verso.

Deming, David. (2010) *Science and Technology in World History, Volume 1: The Ancient World and Classical Civilization*. London: McFarland & Company, Inc.

Descartes, Rene. (1954) *Philosophical Writings: A Selection*. Elizabeth Anscombe and Peter Geach eds. London: Nelson.

Dhanani, Alnoor. (2002) 'Islam'. In Gary B. Ferngren, ed. *Science and Religion: A Historical Introduction*, 73–92. London: Johns Hopkins University Press.

Donald, Merlin. (2013) 'Mimesis Theory Re-Examined, Twenty Years after the Fact'. In Gary Hatfield and Holly Pittman, eds. *Evolution of Mind, Brain, and Culture*, 169–192. Philadelphia: University of Pennsylvania Museum of Archaeology and Anthropology.

Goff, Philip. (2019) *Galileo's Error: Foundations for a New Science of Consciousness*. New York: Pantheon.

Gray, Asa. (1887) *The Elements of Botany for Beginners and Schools*. New York: Ivison.

Guthrie, Stewart E. (1995) *Faces in the Clouds: A New Theory of Religion*. Oxford: Oxford University Press.

Harrison, Peter. (1998) *The Bible, Protestantism, and the Rise of Modern Science*. Cambridge: Cambridge University Press.

Heelas, Paul and Linda Woodhead. (2005) *The Spiritual Revolution: Why Religion Is Giving Way to Spirituality*. Oxford: Blackwell.

Henry, John. (2010) 'Religion and the Scientific Revolution'. In Peter Harrison, ed. *The Cambridge Companion to Science and Religion*, 39–58. Cambridge: Cambridge University Press.

Hill, Faith. (2019) 'They Tried to Start a Church Without God. For a While, It Worked', *The Atlantic*, available at: www.theatlantic.com/ideas/archive/2019/07/secular-churches-rethink-their-sales-pitch/594109.

Hoffmeier, James K. (2015) *Akhenaten and the Origins of Monotheism*. Oxford: Oxford University Press.

Kirk, G. S., J. E. Raven, and M. Schofield. (1983) *The Presocratic Philosophers*. Cambridge: Cambridge University Press.

Laland, Kevin M. (2017) *Darwin's Unfinished Symphony: How Culture Made the Human Mind*. Princeton, NJ: Princeton University Press.

Lewens, Tim. (2017) *Cultural Evolution: Conceptual Challenges*. Oxford: Oxford University Press.

Lindberg, David C. (2002) 'Medieval Science and Religion'. In Gary B. Ferngren, ed. *Science and Religion: A Historical Introduction*, 57–72. London: Johns Hopkins University Press.

Martin, David. (2011) *The Future of Christianity: Reflections on Violence and Democracy, Religion and Secularization*. Burlington, VT: Ashgate.

Nagel, Thomas. (2012) *Mind and Cosmos: Why the Materialist Neo-Darwinian Conception of Nature Is Almost Certainly False*. New York: Oxford University Press.

Norris, Pippa and Ronald Inglehart. (2004) *Sacred and Secular: Religion and Politics Worldwide*. Cambridge: Cambridge University Press.

Osler, Margaret J. (2002) 'Mechanical Philosophy'. In Gary B. Ferngren, ed. *Science and Religion: A Historical Introduction*, 143–152. London: Johns Hopkins University Press.

Paley, William. (1809) *Natural Theology: Or, Evidences of the Existence and Attributes of the Deity*, 12th ed. London: J. Faulder.

Pinker, Steven. (2018) *Enlightenment Now: The Case for Reason, Science, Humanism, and Progress*. New York: Viking.

Price, Michael. (2015) 'The World Needs a Secular Community Revolution', The Evolution Institute, available at: https://evolution-institute.org/the-world-needs-a-secular-community-revolution.

Richerson, Peter J. and Robert Boyd. (2006) *Not by Genes Alone: How Culture Transformed Human Evolution*. Chicago, IL: The University of Chicago Press.

Rosenberg, Alex. (2012) *The Atheist's Guide to Reality: Enjoying Life Without Illusions*. New York: W. W. Norton.

Rupke, Nicolas. (1983) *The Great Chain of History: William Buckland and the English School of Geology, 1814–1849*. Oxford: Oxford University Press.

Ruse, Michael. (2012) *The Philosophy of Human Evolution*. Cambridge: Cambridge University Press.

Schellenberg, J. L. (2007) *The Wisdom to Doubt: A Justification of Religious Skepticism*. Ithaca, NY: Cornell University Press.

Schellenberg, J. L. (2014) 'The End Is Not Near', *Aeon*, available at: https://aeon.co/essays/why-do-we-assume-the-future-will-be-short-blame-the-bible.

Schellenberg, J. L. (2019) *Religion After Science: The Cultural Consequences of Religious Immaturity*. Cambridge: Cambridge University Press.

Searle, John R. (2004) *Mind: A Brief Introduction*. New York: Oxford University Press.

Slone, D. Jason and William W. McCorkle. (2019) *The Cognitive Science of Religion: A Methodological Introduction to Key Empirical Studies*. London: Bloomsbury.

Stromberg, Roland N., ed. (1968) *Realism, Naturalism, and Symbolism: Modes of Thought and Expression in Europe, 1848–1914*. London: Palgrave Macmillan.

Swinburne, Richard. (2004) *The Existence of God*, 2nd ed. Oxford: Oxford University Press.

Swinburne, Richard. (2013) *Mind, Brain, and Free Will*. Oxford: Oxford University Press.

Taylor, Charles. (1991) *The Ethics of Authenticity.* Cambridge, MA: Harvard University Press.

Taylor, Charles. (2007) *A Secular Age.* Cambridge, MA: Harvard University Press.

Wallace, Alfred Russel. (1889) *Darwinism: An Exposition of the Theory of Natural Selection with Some of Its Applications.* London: Macmillan and Co.

Westfall, Richard. (1971) *Force in Newton's Physics: The Science of Dynamics in the Seventeenth Century.* London: Macdonald.

Whitehead, Alfred North. (1929) *Science and the Modern World.* Cambridge: Cambridge University Press.

Wilson, David B. (2002) 'The Historiography of Science and Religion'. In Gary B. Ferngren, ed. *Science and Religion: A Historical Introduction,* 13–29. London: Johns Hopkins University Press.

Woodhead, Linda. (2016) 'The Rise of "No Religion" in Britain: The Emergence of a New Cultural Majority'. *Journal of the British Academy* 4: 245–61.

Wright, Robert. (2009) *The Evolution of God.* New York: Little, Brown and Company.

Websites

www.pewresearch.org/fact-tank/2018/04/25/key-findings-about-americans-belief-in-god

www.pewresearch.org/fact-tank/2018/05/29/10-key-findings-about-religion-in-western-europe

https://gssdataexplorer.norc.org/trends/Religion%20&%20Spirituality?measure=god

www.cnn.com/2019/04/13/us/no-religion-largest-group-first-time-usa-trnd/index.html

www.pewforum.org/2019/10/17/in-u-s-decline-of-christianity-continues-at-rapid-pace

www.atheistallianceamerica.org/meaning-life-research-shift-secular-values

www.pewforum.org/2018/11/20/where-americans-find-meaning-in-life

https://news.gallup.com/poll/1690/religion.aspx

Cambridge Elements⹀

Religion and Monotheism

Paul K. Moser
Loyola University Chicago
Paul K. Moser is Professor of Philosophy at Loyola University Chicago. He is the author of *Understanding Religious Experience*; *The God Relationship*; *The Elusive God* (winner of national book award from the Jesuit Honor Society); *The Evidence for God*; *The Severity of God*; *Knowledge and Evidence* (all Cambridge University Press); and *Philosophy after Objectivity* (Oxford University Press); co-author of *Theory of Knowledge* (Oxford University Press); editor of *Jesus and Philosophy* (Cambridge University Press) and *The Oxford Handbook of Epistemology* (Oxford University Press); co-editor of *The Wisdom of the Christian Faith* (Cambridge University Press). He is the co-editor with Chad Meister of the book series *Cambridge Studies in Religion, Philosophy, and Society*.

Chad Meister
Bethel University
Chad Meister is Professor of Philosophy and Theology and Department Chair at Bethel College. He is the author of *Introducing Philosophy of Religion* (Routledge, 2009), *Christian Thought: A Historical Introduction*, 2nd edition (Routledge, 2017), and *Evil: A Guide for the Perplexed*, 2nd edition (Bloomsbury, 2018). He has edited or co-edited the following: *The Oxford Handbook of Religious Diversity* (Oxford University Press, 2010), *Debating Christian Theism* (Oxford University Press, 2011), with Paul Moser, *The Cambridge Companion to the Problem of Evil* (Cambridge University Press, 2017), and with Charles Taliaferro, *The History of Evil* (Routledge, 2018, in six volumes).

About the Series

This Cambridge Element series publishes original concise volumes on monotheism and its significance. Monotheism has occupied inquirers since the time of the Biblical patriarch, and it continues to attract interdisciplinary academic work today. Engaging, current, and concise, the Elements benefit teachers, researchers and advanced students in religious studies, Biblical studies, theology, philosophy of religion, and related fields.

Cambridge Elements ☰

Religion and Monotheism

Elements in the Series

Buddhism and Monotheism
Peter Harvey

Monotheism and the Meaning of Life
T. J. Mawson

Monotheism and Contemporary Atheism
Michael Ruse

Monotheism and Hope in God
William J. Wainwright

Monotheism and Religious Diversity
Roger Trigg

Divine Ideas
Thomas M. Ward

Hindu Monotheism
Gavin Dennis Flood

Monotheism and the Rise of Science
J. L. Schellenberg

A full series listing is available at: www.cambridge.org/er&m